For those who feel greatness flowing through their blood streams but struggle to embrace it.

"The battles that count aren't the ones for gold medals.

The struggles within yourself—the invisible,

inevitable battles inside all of us—that's where it's at."

— Jesse Owens

Contents

PART 3:

COMMITMENT

Introduction

"The triumph can't be had without the struggle." – Wilma Rudolph

I played 44 games in college and lost 37 of them. Life will surely give you reasons to be disappointed. Tears fell in the team showers as thoughts of what could have been done to win anxiously repeated in my mind. Blame, anger, and hatred for all the things I could not control. "If I only would have..." Ah, damn! "I had it, bro I don't know how I missed that play." Maybe you should have got to practice earlier, maybe you shouldn't have been thinking about how crazy that party was in the film session, and maybe you should have taken those reps at practice more seriously. Or maybe, you should just start getting ready for the next week's game.

Next week's game comes and goes, blown out in the fourth

quarter, no sacks, let up 3 touchdowns. Their team was well-coached and the quarterback was pretty good honestly. "I heard he got a Big Ten offer." "Yeah, he was raw!" Said my starting linebacker. As rage began to fuel up inside me, I somehow decided to agree that this player was that much better than me--that they just had it, talent, and good coaches--and I didn't. "Damn, was he that much better," I thought, sitting at the dining hall table with my teammates laughing and joking about the loss. Why was I so angry? Why was I still upset about this play? Why was I looking up this quarterback's offers out of high school? I watched his interviews and looked at his stats. There was no way I was that bad: maybe it was my cleats, they'd been slipping in practice too, and I should've changed them out before the game started. "I'm definitely getting new cleats for next week, can't wait for next week against Villanova," I decided.

The long bus ride back the following week was somber. We were blown out by 21 points, no sacks, taken out in the fourth quarter. New cleats were still on my feet. This time they had a running back who was really good--at least, that what the coach whispered before the game. "Yeah bro, he was fast, his jersey was mad tight, couldn't catch him!" My teammates went back and forth on the bus. 0-9 on the season, my sophomore year was going absolutely terrible. This was a nightmare.

I held back tears of disappointment in the team film session watching myself give up big plays. My ego shot down, I felt worthless. I hoped and prayed false prayers that the coach wouldn't call me out in front of my teammates for a lack of effort and leadership. As I watched myself on film, I realized that I looked tired and undisciplined. I seemed unprepared and uncertain of my responsibility. I was not helping my team win. I admitted to myself that I wasn't part of the solution: I was part of the problem.

I was part of the problem. This has been the greatest realization of my life, leading me to try to understand why I was part of the problem instead of the solution. I have always believed that I was capable of being a part of the solution, but unfortunately the reality was that I needed to find a solution to the most important problem first: myself. I learned the problem wasn't on the outside, but rather deeply embedded into my mind and how I dealt with disappointment.

You know that feeling of wanting to do so well that you can't even imagine any other scenario than you crushing it? You show up each day with the intention to get better, you make all the necessary sacrifices--at least, you think. In your heart you know you want to excel, you have been putting things in place, you have done all the necessary steps that are supposed to equate success and fulfillment. Your family is rooting for you, or at least they are supposed to. You're focused, or at least you're expected to be. You have lived those moments in your mind over and over, you got this, or you may not have it at all. It begins to feel like you are fighting yourself everyday and there are no signs of either side winning. But, eventually, there is a winner because this type of battle has no room for two victors. The battle is fought between high expectations and our response to self disappointment.

I've chosen to include this dialogue to begin this book because conversations with myself and others have become my coping mechanism over time. My team and I weren't successful at winning in college, leading to many of us living with self-doubt, complaining, and disappointment. Throughout those four years, I needed to find a way to cope, accept the losses, and move on. I never entirely could admit that I wasn't good enough or didn't possess the capabilities to be. My teammates were good men, talented and hardworking, but we struggled to produce wins for the program.

Even after the years of losses and few wins, I remain grateful for the opportunity to be where I was in life; you will read more about why later on in this book. The game of football has played an enormous part in my development. My time spent playing growing up has undoubtedly contributed to the expectations I have for myself today. I have faced numerous difficult decisions, overcame discomfort, and found a way to build and execute. Football has also contributed to my feelings of self-disappointment. Many times I punished myself for poor performance and lost my confidence about my ability to play. It's safe to say; I've felt every emotion on my journey and still have moments today that are unsettling.

At only 25 years of age, I find myself reflecting on my life quite often. I am convinced that as humans, we are the result of patterns. These patterns are obvious to see for many of us, and for others, it may not be as clear. Identifying my patterns of behavior over the years has created a need to understand myself. If I'm honest, it is taking me some time to accept all the disappointment. I always prided myself on understanding my surroundings, people, and circumstance. For me, these things were a result of my ability to communicate with others.

Today, my primary focus has been to finally understand the most important but yet most complicated individual in my life: ME. I've begun my fight there. This fight has been a signal that the battle within is finally starting. We all will encounter this signal at some point, or multiple time in our life. However, you can be confident that this fight within ourselves is the most important one.

In these pages, you will read about a journey with self disappointment and high expectations: a journey I'm sure that you too have experienced and maybe are still experiencing. I aim to encourage you to reflect, and in that reflection, I hope to provide you with perspective on how to overcome your own disappointment and strive freely.

Writing this book has been one of the most difficult things I've done in my life because the self disappointment has taken me to some dark places. Many times I stopped to address my emotional state as the truth spilled onto the paper.

But, here it is anyway. Thank you for taking the time to read it.

SELF AWARENESS

Chapter 1:

Tough Love

"Good job son." - Dad

His wrist bracelets jangled in my left ear as he patted me twice on the back with a tight shoulder squeeze. My dad has some massive hands, and you know he is coming the moment you hear those bracelets begin hitting one another.

"Junior, you gotta sack that quarterback!" He would say in his strong west Indian voice after every game. To him, it didn't matter if I got the sack or not. He would still criticize me or encourage me to do more. He was one of those dads that just wanted to show you support even if his knowledge of what he was supporting was vague. I suppose that was the reality of almost every immigrant parent attempting to understand American sports. The "good job son" was almost always followed by two cheeseburgers, large fries, and a medium Sprite with a lot of ice from McDonald's on Nevins Street in Downtown Brooklyn. Not many words followed after the game, but a number 2 from McDonald's told me that my dad was proud. My brother Raheem and I knew exactly what being disappointed looked like, so moments like these we knew to enjoy. My dad is the most positive and friendly man I know. However, his kids, as Coach Bill would say, were "some damn knuckleheads."

Whatever gene parents pass down to their children that makes them obedient, respectful, and disaster-proof seemed to remove itself from our DNA. In return for displaying the extent of our knuckle headedness, we were disciplined regularly. For those who may be unfamiliar, "lix" was a form of discipline that somehow resulted in amazing sleep afterward. It is reasonable to say Raheem and I were "badass kids". There came a point where both of us became too much for any one family which resulted in my brother leaving to live with my biological mother when I was 14 years old.

The freedom from parental discipline ended for him but continued at an all-time high for me. It became very evident that I was capable of holding up my end alone. I was loved and I knew I was loved with each lash from the belt. Love and pain had a powerful relationship that I learned early on. It hurt my dad deeply to discipline me in that manner, but you give your children what you know, and he knew that poor outputs had consequences. He understood that it was up to him to provide the foundation for good outputs and discipline poor ones. Today I'm confident to state that it worked, because I now know the difference. I have such a profound understanding of the difference between them that it has been deeply embedded in my mind over the years. I know that good outputs are merely expectations and poor outputs are followed by discipline. Isn't that how society is structured? If a cop pulls you over and you're wearing your seatbelt, then the focus becomes something else wrong with your driving. If your seatbelt isn't on, then that is then added to the list of issues. We are wired to identify the problem, we are human-- we problem solve.

"Thank you for wearing your seatbelt tonight, here is your ticket for that illegal turn," is never said. It's not the cops fault; his salary is not predicated on two pats on the back and a tight squeeze on the shoulder, or a good job son. When a "knucklehead" does the right thing, those who they have burdened treat it as a sign of relief. The expectation had been set that Duncan's kids were prone to messing stuff up and doing the wrong thing. I didn't want to carry the reputation as a kid who just messed things up, so I became very good at punishing poor outputs myself. There wasn't a belt larger than the one I used on myself. Mastering the art of depriving myself of the two cheeseburgers, large fries, and the Sprite with a lot of ice was easy. The deprivation felt necessary, though somehow I would still look forward to at least the large fries. I tasted it, smelled it, and planned for what needed to be done to get it. If I was able to do all the necessary steps then maybe I could get the meal. I would build up such an expectation that I was capable of getting myself that reward: I was worthy.

Finally, I would find a way to generate good output so that everyone would tell me, "good job," and indicate that a trip to McDonald's should follow. Instantly, in those moments my taste for McDonald's would diminish. The obsession with it disgusted me and I felt nothing. Depriving myself of the reward for my efforts was way too familiar and comforting that there came a time when there was no McDonald's, not even a trip downtown. The metaphors I am referring to is the reward and how I didn't allow myself to enjoy good things because I felt I wasn't deserving of them.

The shoulder squeezes from my dad began feeling unnecessary and the bracelets on his wrist were loud and annoying. The "good job son"no longer validated me. It wasn't my dad's fault--it was mine. Our minds are paramount. It is like we all have our own personal Hulk in us. The force is so powerful that it will take control of you when failed to contain. It's going to take years of work to even keep it from killing you, and after you've learned that, the work only begins. Our mind needs to be fed often, played with regularly, and given fresh air. Frequent stimulation is imperative. If it does not receive these basic needs, it will play games with us, control us, pick and choose when to give us peace. It will likely do its best to adapt to any situation regardless of how traumatic the experience is.

THANK YOU BRAIN

I've had five diagnosed concussions by the age of 22. I owe my brain a lifetime of gratitude for giving me the strength to write this book. I'm working on earning its forgiveness for consistently depriving it of reward, and at times it reminds me of that. I know some of you may be thinking that I sound a bit insane but many of you will know what I mean. "Tough love" has built up resilience, hard work, and a never-say-die attitude, and those things have opened many doors for me. However, punishment has been simply too harsh, too often. If I never learned to balance the response to the outputs in my life, then I would have run the risk of taking the highway to ultimate self-destruction.

In a research article written by a professor at Cornell University, it mentioned that people who seem strong enough may inflict pain on themselves to balance their misdeeds. In a search to understand why I was so "messed up", I would learn that feeling like I let myself down was my way of balancing the scales. This way of thinking created a need to balance the scales constantly. If things were going poorly, I would seek escape routes and excitement. If things were going too well, I would punish myself for not creating resistance. This cycle was never-ending, and sadly, extremely easy to hide. I hid it by becoming a "go-getter", having a "never satisfied attitude", and saying things like "I got this" and "I'm just focused right now". All these statements have very positive energies connected to them as well.

Someone referred to as a go-getter is normally a great thing, has the confidence to say "I got this", and actually possesses the willpower to prove it is celebrated. I'm not suggesting that my use of these phrases and terms was negative at all because I am a hard worker and I strive for excellence daily. The variable that separates how I was using them and how others do was the intentions behind their usage. There is absolutely nothing wrong with being a go- getter, but I used it to hide the fact that I was unappreciative of positive outcomes in my life. I realized that MAYBE I had a problem. I emphasize maybe because the issues that I perceived to be negative may not be an issue for another individual. Some may even suggest there is nothing wrong with a "never satisfied attitude". Growing up as a football player allowed me to disguise my lack of gratitude. It gave me the perfect cover-up for secretly not caring about positive outcomes. I hid it so well for many years that it was only recently that I began to hear the whispers and decided to make a change. Back in high school when the team got a great win, everyone would be in the locker room celebrating. But there I was, secretly wishing we lost so everyone would stay "hungry". Deep down, I wanted everyone to be more humble so that we could get back to working harder. I would be as tired as the rest of my teammates after playing a full football game. Collectively, we would do anything to win: as brothers we fought, protected each other, made plays, and finished strong. I deserved every right to celebrate and jump around filled with joy in the locker room, but I wasn't. The smell of 50 sweaty football players in a locker room was certainly one that I have smelled dozens of times and have always embraced. After winning our 4th straight game of the season, the morale of the team was high, coaches were happy, fans and parents could not stop bragging about us. We were celebrities at school, and all the girls wanted to hang out with us. We were off to a legendary start. We didn't allow any team to score on us. We worked hard, and personally I was having my best season so far. So why the hell was I not happy and singing along at the top of my lungs with the rest of my teammates?

The smell of the locker room angered me. I was out of place and undeserving of my starting role on the team. I felt so confused so I decided to hide this type of thinking. After all, I figured they were just thoughts. Smiling and laughing when approached was effortless, hanging out after the game receiving all the praise was routine. I normally had the longest commute home out of anyone on the team, which gave me time to think about all the things I didn't do right during the games. I finally had time to feel nothing, just another day. I would go home and my dad would have to ask me about the game before I said anything about it. I would forget that I had even played an entire football game that afternoon.

Convinced that this type of thinking and behavior meant that I was just that much more focused than others, I allowed it to repeat throughout the season. It wasn't long before the guilt of all the negative thoughts began to feel heavier. I wasn't negative with my teammates at all--if you asked any one of them today, they would say I was almost always joking and having a good time. I felt extremely different and alone almost every day of school and practice.

Do you know that feeling when you feel you can't relate to anyone? Conversations and debates about popular topics amongst my peers were no place for me. The loneliness was real. When someone who you love shows you "tough love", you know they want the best for you and they are helping build your character. It may suck in that moment and hurt your feelings, but the hope is that you come out tougher and more resilient. These things I know, but I knew nothing of the impact of tough love on myself. I told myself that no one was going to be harder on me than I was on myself, so I didn't need anyone else's help figuring it out. Before someone could tell me that I was wrong, I was trying to make it right. Telling me how I could make it right would have been a monumental waste of breath: "I got this."

I am a team player. I have been voted captain of every team I have ever been on, and loved every moment of playing the beautiful game of football. However tearing myself down, pouring salt in my wounds, and kicking myself until I bled was MY JOB! I wouldn't let anyone, I didn't care who you were, to take the power of punishing me away from me. For a long time, this was cool, and I hid it well under my "hard worker" shell. I became the poster boy for how to work hard and show up early and get after it.

COACH LANDBERG

Coach Landberg was my high school football head coach. He came and recruited me from my pee-wee team to be part of what he has now created, which is nothing short of a high school football dynasty in NYC. He stood about 5 foot 5 inches tall but he walked like he was a giant. He spoke with certainty, he loved his players, and we loved him. He had that kind of tough love that would make you climb a mountain just to meet him at the top. When he said to do something, you did that no questions asked. He took average players, troubled kids, kids who were in jail, quiet kids, and anyone he could find that can play an ounce of football and made them winners. My 1 1/2 hour commute every morning for 4 years was worth it because to play for Coach Landberg meant to do whatever needed to be done to show up.

Have you ever had that one person in your life that you didn't want to disappoint because of how much they meant to your growth? He was the embodiment of this for me, and I still get nervous today even speaking with him. I disappointed Coach Landberg dozens of times because I never unlearned the "knucklehead" title I was given. The guilt was unbearable and I quite literally spent my entire junior and senior season trying to earn his forgiveness.

"Jose Duncan is one of the hardest-working players I have ever coached," he said during the senior year banquet. It took a lot of discipline but eventually I earned his forgiveness and that of all my other coaches, but forgiving myself wasn't a priority. So while I would kill it on the field, my grades and my behavior was mediocre. This was the only place where I was not hard on myself at all, it was *"Alll good"*.

WAKE UP MOMENT

Punishment from my father simply wore off the moment I would return to school the following day. If it wasn't lunchtime or gym period, you had about a 20% chance of getting my attention. Self-discipline didn't exist there, and I didn't care. When college coaches visited the school asking about me as a prospect, I was the best student in the class on those days.

The conversations with the scouts would be great, they

loved me, but I never got an offer. One day during my junior year, I asked Coach Landberg why he didn't get back to me about offers from any coaches; he laughed. "You're not going anywhere with your grades Jose, get out my office!" He said this as if he believed I was joking by asking. Sitting on the top floor of the staircase, I began to cry and sob. My chest was hurting, and I was shaking. I had never felt that disappointed in myself and alone ever in my life before that moment. I spent 2 hours in that staircase, I knew nobody would come up here because this was the spot where a few of us would come to smoke and chill with girls during classes. Only a few people knew about this spot because it was a door that we left propped open for each other. I knew it was safe to cry here, in the very same place I would be instead of learning. Hanging out and cutting classes here was a ritual. Everyone who spent time in that spot had poor academic standings, didn't talk about life after high school and future dreams. I had no one to blame. I probably wasn't going to college, and my parents couldn't afford it. I fucked up.

Moments like these have been monumental for my life. Being alone and crying in that stairway taught me what isolation truly felt like. The same guys I would hang out with to fit in weren't there when I was at my lowest point: I had to own my shit. In my senior year, I would take extreme ownership of my future: hanging out with anyone who I didn't feel was on the same path as me was unacceptable. I was focused, disciplined, and motivated more than ever to get to college. Hearing teammates talking about college and offers fueled me, I wanted so badly to join those conversations. I worked out every day, went to all my classes, visited with teachers, and did everything to improve my grades so that I got to college. I showed up to practice early, stayed late, watched the film with coaches, you name it. You would not find a more determined football player in the state of New York. The feeling of taking extreme ownership of my future gave me adrenaline.

The tough love I treated myself with gave me the focus I needed to earn a full scholarship to college. It got me off that staircase junior year. Everyone will agree that discipline is one of the most important skills you will ever practice. No one should want you to succeed more than you want yourself to succeed, and if they do, you are wasting their time. I learned that if you don't want it, not a person in this world can make you want it. Pain is universal. Without hustle and perseverance, the pain will certainly feel like a tranquilizer.

If you are reading this, you have overcome some sort of pain. I know you have willed your way through struggle, overcame your setbacks, and have shown up when it was time to work. You have been tough on yourself, more than any other human could imagine, and to your benefit, it worked, you've made some progress in life and that's a fact. So, why are you still unhappy, unfulfilled, and restless? It's not that you lack satisfaction with your life, it's not that you aren't grateful-- you may be the most grateful person out of all your friends. That tough love you have given yourself has gotten you to this point physically, socially, and maybe even financially, and you're thankful. But the underlying issue is that we never dealt with the guilt from how we treated ourselves over the years. We never forgave ourselves for the letdowns and shortcomings.

Emotionally, we have disabled ourselves; spiritually, we have doubted our faith. Along your journey, you have used up all the bandaids you could find and even attempted to wear clothing to cover it up. The wound never healed, but you dealt with it, and it didn't burn because no one saw it and no one touched it. At times I would watch the scabs on my body try to repair the skin, then, right before they fully healed I would slowly peel it off. The problem with this was, when the wound would be exposed to new trauma, I would forget to cover it up and it would bleed again. In those moments, I would feel extreme disappointment in myself because I knew I was right back where I started.

We experience moments where we feel we have changed or elevated in some capacity, but to our surprise the same problem arises again after all our efforts. It's almost like we convinced ourselves that we changed even though we didn't reach the solution we expected. This can be exhausting, and disappointment usually leaves us confused and emotional. When we find ourselves this way, a lot of us choose to sacrifice self-love and self-healing to become tough and unshakable. Sadly, we get exactly what we wanted, but we don't know it until we are exposed to new circumstances. Healing is a process, and whether you do it now or later, it will need to get done.

· ·

The longer you attempt to avoid the guilt and self- harm you have done onto yourself, the more difficult the healing process will be.

· ·

The tough love has been excessive, and life's circumstances has made this clear to you. Step One is to reflect about all the emotional harm you have caused yourself and simply say, "I'm sorry." Take time to forgive yourself. It will require patience, but you need to forgive yourself. When you finally reach that point, your job isn't over.

Now it's time to forgive others.

Chapter 2:

Who's Fault is It?

"I always fight with my brother. This is our way of saying I love you" – Unknown

My brother and I watched in shock as glass shattered on the floor. We always enjoyed play fighting in the house and the occasional breaking of expensive glassware signaled that playtime was over. When things like this happened, it usually followed with my dad rising out of his La-Z-Boy chair to grab one of his belts. As we always did, we both began to cry and run in opposite directions, and my dad would return with the belt with the big buckle that had a horse molded onto it. My brother and I were frightened because we both knew this particular belt meant he was really upset.

"How did this happen?" he yelled.

"It just fell," my brother cried.

I knew from previous experiences that I now had to support the lie of the glassware just randomly falling, so I did. My dad would ask us three times what happened but we stuck to our lie because that's what siblings do--never give in. My brother got in trouble twice in the last week and now we both were going to get grounded and punished again.

"It was Jose, he was playing and he kicked it and it fell," my brother cried out. "No, it was Raheem!" I replied frantically.

My dad would take his side that day. I got whooped and had to face the wall for two hours. Facing the wall meant that I would stand and stare at the wall with my hands in the air. I couldn't move or put my hands down or I would get in trouble. I am convinced that this form of punishment was why I have such overdeveloped trap muscles today. I wanted to beat my brother up until he started crying. I was so angry and swore to never fight with him again. He broke the bond, he let me down, he gave in.

Staring at the wall, I thought of all the times that we got punished together and how that kept us close, and how this time he let me take the fall. It took me a week to talk to him again. He hurt my feelings and he knew he had let me down. We didn't fight after that day for about two months, but when my dad's birthday came around we would play fight again. I wasn't mad at him anymore, I didn't want to be angry, and I missed playing with my best friend. At a young age I was taught that when it comes to family, nothing is more important. Therefore when someone in your family wrongs you, you have a responsibility to forgive them and move on.

Although we were told these lessons as young teenagers, it was clear that my family didn't display forgiveness for each other very often. There has always been tension between my parents that I never understood. Why they couldn't forgive wasn't a conversation that came up much growing up. My best guess was a lack of communication between two strong personalities.

WE HURT EACH-OTHER SOMETIMES

We all have grudges towards others--how can we not? Some thing feel unforgivable, especially when you love the person. Sometimes the person doesn't know they hurt you, or sometimes they're unaware of how much pain and heartache they caused. However, you are not the victim. This type of behavior is inevitable. Take a moment to reflect on how you may have hurt someone in the past physically or emotionally. Do you know the extent of their pain today? Are you aware of the decisions that followed that pain and how it impacted their lives?

Newton's Third Law states that, *"for every action, there is an equal and opposite reaction."* Let's take a moment to appreciate being human. We can take a life and save a life all in the same day. It's remarkable to think about the power we have to influence reactions in this world. If one person makes a poor decision, in some way that decision will impact millions of people differently whether they know it or not. As a human race, we try to reduce the spread of negative decisions while magnifying the impact of positive ones. Therefore, we all are simply sharing negative and positive energy all the time without fail. The first step to forgiving the negative energy that someone shared with you is to question their intent. We must understand the underlying reason why a person acted in that particular behavior towards us. Was their intent to hurt us? What might have influenced that person's decision? How well do we know this particular individual and is this behavior uncommon? These are all important questions to ask ourselves. Questions like these will lead to better communication when addressing that individual. The goal of this book is to teach you ways to stop letting yourself down without sacrificing your standards. Therefore, learning how to protect your peace is mandatory. This step of the process is about communicating with those who hurt you so that you can begin practicing forgiveness.

THE WORST KIND OF PAIN

Regret is one of the most emotionally painful things to find peace with. Watching my mother's lifeless body in her casket triggered the most regret I have ever felt in my life. For many years, I blamed my mom for not being involved in my life. I blamed her for not disciplining my brother when he went to live with her. Teenage freedom and lack of discipline at home led to him spending time incarcerated for making one too many mistakes. She didn't call much and when I went to visit her I didn't feel the love I expected. Love is complicated, and I'm certain that being a parent is even more complicated. My dad and mom had their differences, and my brother and I knew that they couldn't even tolerate each other. I longed for a better relationship with my mother, and at times I felt as if I was the blame for not reaching out to her. I was always told that we had so much in common, and the few times I was able to spend time with my mom, the connection was seldom. I knew that she was a messy eater, always spilling food on herself when she ate--that was me all the way. I certainly had her smile and our eyes were almost identical.

I started to think that maybe it was my fault; perhaps I should have reached out to her more as a teenager. I often pondered about her not taking of my brother. I felt so disappointed in her. "How could she not look after Raheem?" I thought to myself often. My brother being incarcerated was something I solely blamed on her. As the years went on, I became more angry and confused, and I never found a way to forgive her. My heart felt heavy as I stood there staring at her lifeless body, I started whispering, "I'm sorry, I'm sorry." I didn't want anyone at the funeral to hear the regret in my voice. There was so much left unsaid and unsettled. I waited until the funeral was over and everyone left so I could go back inside to see her one last time to say "I forgive you, mom".

That day I forgave her for not calling to ask me how football was going. As a kid, I wanted to know that she was proud of me because I kept out of trouble. "Keeping out of trouble" for young black kids growing up in the inner city was a win like no other. I forgave her for not disciplining poor outputs by my brother the way my dad did for me. She wasn't my dad, so it was wrong for me to hold her to the same standards: her circumstances were very different. I forgave her for all things that I felt prior to that moment were unforgivable because at the end of her life she didn't deserve to be hated. My mother didn't deserve my pain. Her struggles and perceived failures in life were her own to bear and I didn't need to remind myself of how it impacted me. That day my attitude shifted to appreciation. I appreciated who she was or wasn't because I grew from it.

I knew my mom's intentions were not to hurt me all those years: I was her son. I knew her enough to know that she loved me, and I knew that she was dealing with her misfortunes in life. Those misfortunes may have led her not to be the best mother to my brother, and I understand that now. My brother grew up too fast, and the unfortunate part was that this wasn't uncommon in black families. Through it all, I still believe my mother tried her best. She gave me life and an opportunity to live in this beautiful world. It took me several years to stop regretting my hatred for my mother, but today I have found peace with it. I try maintaining my peace of mind by reminding myself that she was human and humans make mistakes. I forgave her that day and took power back; I decided to own my pain. Today, it's my responsibility to learn from her mistakes. It's not okay for me to make those same mistakes when I get the opportunity to raise my children.

Remember, you are human, and the person that hurt you is human as well. We all make mistakes. It is entirely normal to be angry. Anger is a reaction to someone's actions, and the significant part about it is that we're in control of our responses. While you feel anger, that person may be feeling guilt, and guilt can lead to more harm to oneself than anger. Is there someone that you hurt? Are they still feel angry about it? What was the catalyst that leads to the disagreement? Who deserves the blame? The truth is it doesn't matter who's at fault because now, both of you are living with negative emotions about that situation. Choosing not to forgive leaves us carrying a heavy burden, and now you both are carrying that negative energy everywhere. Once the anger and guilt subsides, the energy remains and it will never truly go unless we take the necessary step. Unlike my situation, the person who hurt you may still be alive and reachable, and it may be time to begin your journey to forgiving them. The forgiveness is not for them, it's for you, and it is available to you.

We all know that life is short, and each passing of people we love reminds us of this timeless fact. As true a statement as it is, unfortunately, many of you will continue to carry that pain because forgiveness it's not easy and never will be. Fear of judgment will keep you from picking up the phone, but this step is necessary. You CANNOT skip this step, it doesn't matter if you think you don't care or are convinced that it doesn't bother you anymore. It is necessary. Protect your long term peace, decide to forgive, and watch how it changes your life.

••

It doesn't matter what powers you may feel you possess-- correcting the past is beyond our capabilities.

••

Once you have decided to take this step in your growth process and look toward the future, you are golden.

There will be a key step that you will need to maximize your relationship with yourself and others, and the step I'm referring to is effective communication.

Chapter 3:

If We Only Communicated Better

"Being able to communicate with people is power" - Oprah
Winfrey

In a football locker room, there are very few things that aren't allowed. It's one of the few places I've ever been that gives all participants the freedom to be themselves and the freedom to express one's thoughts. Guys would say all kinds of whacked out stuff. Conversations would range from things like sports, girls, money, school, comedy, and even politics. It was a nonjudgmental space and I loved it. In my opinion, a sports locker room is one of the most sacred places in the world. Very few outsiders know what goes on in there, but if you have ever been a member of one, you should have an idea.

However, there was one thing that was a sin in the locker room. This behavior was not accepted because if allowed, it would spread like cancer. When a player was caught doing it, it was called out immediately, and as much as it hurt that person it created a stronger brotherhood. It was a sin to talk negatively about a teammate to another teammate, an absolute SIN! In any organization you are a part of, avoid this type of behavior because it will lead to a less cohesive unit, and problem-solving will be almost impossible.

As a college football team, we felt that respect and honesty amongst each other would help us perform better. If there was ever an instance where someone sinned, we would call a team meeting in the middle of the locker room to resolve it. If players were angry at each other, we would allow it to cool down until the time was right to communicate. It didn't matter where it took place--for us to be cohesive, communicating the conflict openly was mandatory. The topic of politics wasn't a normal conversation in the locker room and when it did arise, the debates were brief. We all came from different communities and belief systems but the love of football brought us together.

One day, our starting strong safety and our starting kicker got in a heated debate about political views and right from wrong. The argument was pretty intense as only three lockers separated them. Still, to this day I am very thankful that the teammates sitting in between those lockers tried to deescalate the situation. After that day, they wouldn't come to terms or talk about their differences.

Once after practice, a few of us began to hear chatter: white teammates were talking about black teammates and how they felt targeted and uncomfortable. Not only was this chatter, it became such a conflict in the locker room that the coaches even heard about it. As a team, when you allow coaches to be informed about internal locker room issues then you know something must be done internally to fix the problem. Our coach believed in mass disciplining-- everyone on the team suffered from individual mistakes, and rightfully so, we were a team. Recognizing that this chatter had caused separation in the locker room and poor performance on the field, a few of the team's leaders organized a player's only meeting. The meeting was directly after practice, everyone showed up. It didn't matter if you had class after, you were expected to be present when the meeting began. We locked the doors: coaches nor other team personnel were allowed in our sacred space. A few minutes passed where no one said anything, and then guys started to speak up about what had been said and how they felt about words that had been said. A few guys rebutted and some arguments began to arise. Quickly recognizing what was going on one of my teammates yelled out "YO!! This shit is stupid, who gives a fuck what the arguments are about, we are a team and all that separation and gathering in groups to talk about shit is killing us!"

We agreed, but the tension was still high so we decided to settle the primary issue between the two individuals who had the issue with each other the best way we knew how.

GLOVES ON, CLEAR THE MIDDLE

One minute on the clock, two pairs of boxing gloves, no fighting after knockdowns. These were the rules and they were not to be broken under no circumstances. One of my teammates always kept a pair of gloves in the bottom of his locker for occasions like these. The gloves normally killed two birds with one stone: the dispute gets settled and the rest of us are entertained.

So they began to box. The anger in both of their faces was evident, and they desperately wanted to hurt each other. Both teammates got good punches and even some blood was shed. It was one of the longest minutes I had ever experienced in my life. We were banging on the lockers each time a punch connected. We were young contact sport athletes so we enjoyed the physicality of boxing very much. Many punches didn't land, and it might've been a good thing they didn't connect because from where we all stood, they looked like knockout blows.

When the alarm rang and the fight was over, we could see

the exhaustion in both their faces. We would wait until the tension was a bit lighter before forcing them to hug it out. From that day forward, it became a spoken rule to never again speak about political views in the locker room. I cannot tell you who won the fight because I respect both men, and I am happy to have shared a locker room with them. I, too, have worn the gloves to settle disputes with teammates but it has never been about winning and losing amongst my brothers.

Although, many times the communication took place with two pairs of boxing gloves in the middle of the locker room, once it was over, everything would return to normal. Effectively communicating with others about your disagreement with them is not an easy decision, but an important one nonetheless. Many will argue that physical confrontations aren't effective communication, and in most cases, I agree. However, where most of us came from, it was almost second nature to fight. Today I think we could've handled things differently, but those 1-minute fights established expectations while growing as a team. Establishing future expectations after both sides have been acknowledged is one of the most vital things to practice, and it can come in many forms. Understanding this will help us communicate freely without fear of being misunderstood and misjudged. To effectively communicate with others there are some prerequisites that must happen first.

Think about a time in your life you have seen or

experienced someone displaying poor communication skills. What did it look like? What was the reaction of those involved and what resulted because of it? If the individual had a strong argument to support what they were communicating about it wouldn't matter in this case. Poor communication is still communication because there is an exchange, someone is giving and the other receiving. However, the problem will not get solved, or it will take longer than expected to be resolved. I am placing my emphasis on effective communication because this type of communication will solve your problems and have you feeling a lot less let down. We are all humans, and we will certainly let you down. You can increase your chances of not experiencing such a high degree of disappointment if you learn better communication skills. Provide others with clarity, be clear about the importance of their support. While it's impossible to completely avoid disappointment, lack of communication would be amongst the issues. Experiencing poor communication in any form is a prerequisite because to truly grasp what's effective we need a clear understanding of what's ineffective.

COACH "C"

My collegiate defensive line coach in many ways quickly became one of my role models. 6'3 white guy from Ohio who knew his stuff about becoming a baller and a better man. He was a family man and lived a simple life. He wasn't a simple man but we all knew his priorities were simple: his wife, his children, and his players. He coached me hard, and in his eyes I could see his passion for football. He coached with his heart, and for that, he has earned a lifetime of respect from me. Our relationship was unique; after two years of coaching me I became the leader of my position group and our conversations shifted drastically. We spoke like equal adults. We spoke less about football and more and more about life, the future and family. I was intrigued by how he would carry himself and interact with others--he certainly was an alpha. What I appreciated most was how we communicated. Both he and I knew that he was in charge and I was not, but he gave me space to be "THE GUY".

Coach C was very clear about his expectations for me as a player and a leader, and when I wasn't living up to his expectations he would always pull me aside. A lot like Coach Landberg was for me in high school, Coach C had that same presence about him that made me want to do everything I could to not disappoint him. Mondays were what the football world calls install day; this day is the first day preparing the game plan for the next opponent. One Monday while sitting in the film room at 6:30 am, he said: "Jose, this week we got a mobile quarterback and I need you to have eye control going through your progression this week." After he said that, he didn't refer to me again the entire film session--he would coach other players. He would do this often, give me simple instructions and not refer to me again.

After a while, I began to dislike when he stopped critiquing my performance in practice. I wanted to get better, and I needed his feedback. I remember after one of the worst practices in my junior year I was expecting the coach to call me out in the film room and tell me how much better he expected out of me. I felt guilty because the film would show my lack of effort and that was uncharacteristic for me. That evening in the film room coach would never call my name, it left me disconcerted. He commented on every guy in the room and their practice that day. I sat there with my eyes gazed on the back of his head wondering if he even cared. Hoping to get some constructive feedback, I asked him if he could let me know what I was supposed to do on a particular play. This was how I tried to get his attention: asking for coaching was a way players made sure the coach still wanted the best for them. He would simply say "I've seen you do this better," and say nothing more after that. I became frustrated, approval or disapproval, I didn't care. I just wanted something, anything!

As time passed, he would stop calling out my mistakes on film, and in practice we exchanged little to no words. One day after practice, I went to his office to ask him why he had stopped coaching me so hard. I was disappointed that he didn't call me out when I made mistakes like he did when I was a freshman and sophomore. I felt jealous and left out. I feared that because there were a lot of new guys, he had given up on me because he wanted to focus on the underclassmen.

That day we had a tough practice in the rain and the defensive line gave up some big plays. Everyone knew the head coach wasn't pleased with Coach C. Based on how the post-practice huddle went, it was clear that he was on edge. I walked into his office while he was watching that morning's practice. He still had his raincoat on and mud tracks all over his carpet floor. I could tell he hadn't eaten or got a chance to collect himself after practice, maybe this was a bad time. I always felt nervous walking in his office, because I knew as wise as he was I wouldn't leave his office the way I came in.

After taking ten minutes of his time to explain how I felt, he sat there and we looked at each other. The stare down lasted about 10 seconds. My throat felt dry and my legs couldn't stop shaking underneath me. I was relieved that I found enough courage to express how I felt but I couldn't help feeling like I was complaining. I'd let him know that I feared if he didn't coach me hard, my performance as a player would decline. Without taking his eyes off me, he uttered three words. Those three words he told me that day led me to have one of my best seasons ever and even receiving 3rd Team All CAA, it was a great accomplishment.

"I trust you," he said.

The moment he said it, I felt a wave of emotions flowing through me. Do you know that feeling of not wanting to let someone down but instead of them being disappointed, they tell you that they're proud of you? The only other man in my life to ever tell me those words was my father, and Coach C didn't know it, but he was like a second dad to me. He explained how he trusted me because he knew my intent was to be a good player, he told me that he knew what I wanted as a player and respected me for it. He explained how just giving me simple instructions worked for me and he didn't have to talk down to me because he knew how hard I was on myself. Coach C was always clear about what he needed from me and we spent the previous two years building the foundation that gave me the tools to do my job.

The phrase "DO YOUR JOB" was posted in big letters on the locker room doors and as players, we knew the importance of those words. I learned that for Coach C to not disappoint the head coach, his players, or most importantly himself, he had to be an effective communicator. He needed to have a clear understanding of himself and what his value was to the organization. Only then was he able to communicate clearly to his player what his performance expectations were. He would put us in the best position to succeed because if we performed below team expectations, he knew the blame was on him. I admired him because he took extreme ownership of us as a group, he would coach his players so that we all had a mutual interest in performing well on Saturdays. My disappointment with Coach C was in all actuality the disappointment I had with myself. I didn't trust myself as much as he trusted me. That year we broke the school record for performance on the defensive line and the coach gave us a lot of praise for making him look really good. That season, Coach C showed me the second most important thing for effective communication: understand the personal interests of those you are communicating with.

He spent two years understanding me as a young man and as a football player, therefore he knew how to communicate with me to help me reach my full potential. Placing an emphasis on understanding the interests of those who you communicate with will save you a lot of disappointment and blame. If we do not place a priority on establishing clear expectations when communicating, then we enable others to let us down. As I have mentioned previously, people will let you down. Although you cannot prevent feelings of disappointment, it is possible to increase your chances of fulfillment when someone gives you what you asked for. Step one in the communication process was understanding exactly what effective communication is.

Now, with my help I hope that you can understand your audience and create mutual interest. Throughout the entire process we must remain reasonable with ourselves and most importantly others. Being reasonable is not a step, but a guiding principle of communication.

Many years ago I read a powerful quote that influenced me to live my life with gratitude and humility, which have allowed me to create lifelong connections and strive freely without worry.

· ·

"Life is fair because it's unfair to everyone."

· ·

If you haven't gotten a hold of your ego, this quote may not impact you at all. Honestly when I first read it, I wasn't impacted either. It was hard to truly believe that life was that unfair for everyone. I used to think that there was no way a rich man and a poor man experienced the same unfairness, and many people can likely agree with that statement. As a black man, I felt as if life was more unfair for me more than other races. Slavery and generational oppression have certainly created a level of unfairness that is unmatched. Today I still feel strongly about life being unfair for different populations of people due to a lack of resources, education, and income. However, I also feel strongly about not falling victim to circumstance and how to use the unfairness of life to my advantage.

I am fortunate enough to write this book and you are equally as fortunate to be able to read it. Adapting to the mindset that life is unfair for everyone gave me a greater sense of gratitude for what I had. I wouldn't judge another person for being rich, happy, sad, or poor--instead, I would simply believe that I was in control of my own life and thus my happiness. Many things are out of my control, therefore I became good at controlling the things I can control and letting go of the burden of the uncontrollable occurrences of life, but it wasn't easy.

My lifelong fear of letting down the people I looked up to only led me to let them down even more. I had yet learned the importance of being reasonable with myself and others, and so I would let disappointment tear away at my mind. If a coach asked me to play my best, I automatically assumed he meant to not make any mistakes and to play a perfect game. If my boss asked me to help a customer at work, I would leave my department to help that customer for the next 30 minutes. My standards and personal expectations are high and I will never lower them, but I never left any room for reason. I assumed that others understood me, and I would automatically assume that others should live up to my standards and the way I did things. This type of thinking made me a poor communicator and a less effective leader amongst my peers. My ego was not checked, I allowed it to have its voice, energy, and language, and the person I wanted to be took a back seat. The notion of "if you want something done right, do it yourself" became a constant in my life and it was extremely exhausting.

I have been around many groups of people in my life and I have never met someone who can do everything with no help or assistance, but here I was stretching myself thin routinely. Have you ever felt like it was you who people called upon to "save the day"? If you have, then you know what I mean when I say that there are only so many times you can wear a cape and run into a burning building. Some of us are certainly capable, and it's a gift from the universe to be that person. Unfortunately, the sad truth is that it will lead to no one ever expecting you to be the one who needs saving from that burning building. This was the reason my coach told me he trusted me. He was a reasonable man and he allowed me to get off the ground without his help when I got knocked down. High expectations did not lead him to wearing my football gear for me and running out on the field to do my job. Instead, he chose clear communication and trust: he sent me in the game knowing that I was going to make a bunch of mistakes along the way. I gave up many plays and at times my discipline on the field was questionable but I grew, got better, and my expectations did as well.

In addition to how we communicate with others, how we communicate with ourselves is equally critical in our developments. How we use self-questioning to achieve this will be addressed in detail in a later chapter. However, the voice of reason will provide a great balance to your voice of ambition. The same mindset applies to effectively communicating with others in your network. Setting high standards for the individuals we communicate with often is necessary, those who we choose to frequently communicate with have a profound impact on our thought process. Spend time understanding them, learn what value you can bring to their lives and what value they bring to yours. Once you've learned their value, practice patience. Space to grow around nonjudgmental supporters will certainly result in that person becoming a valuable asset over time. This is the reward for being a reasonable person and displaying it with your communication. People will recognize that not only are you patient, but understanding as well. When someone is deemed understanding, we are likely to work that much harder so that we don't disappoint them.

Effective communication is the key that unlocks the door to a healthy and abundant relationship with ourselves and others. There is no playbook for "good" communication. We are humans and we are phenomenal at sensing energy, some more than others. Body language, tone and choice of words are all things to be mindful of. Many of us will be misunderstood regardless of our efforts to communicate better, and maintaining positive self talk can be a tall task. However, like anything worth being good at, consistency is necessary.

Remember to keep it real. Genuine feedback and suggestions on how to grow will have a better long-term return.

••

Nobody likes a critic without a solution.

••

Reasonability is best used as a tool for balance: abuse it, and you will lack courage, and discarding it will create a hole that you alone won't be able to fill. If you are ever in a tough place in your life where you are experiencing disappointment because of a lack of effective communication, I encourage you to refer back to this chapter.

Chapter 4:

Me, Myself and My Ego

" I am who I am because I had to become this way"- Anonymous

I was 14 when my dad decided to send my brother to Albany, NY to live with my mother. Dealing with the struggle of raising both of us worsened his already high blood pressure. He felt relieved and would now commit to trying to help my mother financially raise a boy. That was by far one of my toughest days as a young teenager. My step sister was seven years older than me, so I knew she couldn't replace losing my best friend. My brother and I shared a bunked bed since we were 6 and 7 years old, he liked the top bunk and I the bottom. It worked out perfectly: we would play fight and spend hours talking about nothing. Our parents turned a walk-in closet into a bedroom which I would sleep in for the next 8 years alone. The night before he left we both cried. I didn't want him to go, but he wanted to live with mommy because dad was strict and it had brought out the worst in him. He didn't want to go either, but it was as if everyone's minds were made up and the arrangements had already been finalized. That morning we woke up to the warm smell of french toast and the tea kettle singing loudly.

My stepmother was masterful in the kitchen. If she was in the kitchen, it was almost a guarantee that you were going to eat one of the best meals of your life. We became accustomed to this-- we both were tall boys with long limbs and we certainly could eat and never hesitated to do so. That morning, we raced to brush our teeth. My brother and I always rushed through this process. We were hungry and cared very little for this extra pointless step before devouring some french toast and meat omelets. My sister was older and moved with better grace than we did: she was smart and by far the most annoying big sister we ever had, but we love her and she loves us. As we sat at the kitchen table, very few words were exchanged. The mood was calm and no one wanted to talk about the reality of going from a family of five to only four. Later that day, my dad and stepmom would drive Raheem to the Port Authority Bus Station and put him on a direct Greyhound bus to Albany. That was it, he was gone. The house felt empty when they returned. Everything was different and the days became longer and the house was quieter.

A family of four changed everything. Life became so different. A lot of attention was given to me and I hated it. My dad decided it was best to not dismantle the bunk bed yet, which I was happy about. I spent a few days in denial that I was alone. Play fighting myself seemed less fun and whispering at night was no longer a thing. I was alone.

I didn't understand why my dad would do this to me. You just don't take brothers away from each other--it was quite traumatizing. The only person that knew me and accepted who I was was my brother, and now I had to be okay with being alone having no one to share my foolish teenage ideas with. I was afraid.

I always felt bad for the kids who were only children. I always imagined how lonely it must have been for them and how much their parents likely spoiled them. Now that I was alone without a partner to share punishment with, I knew that to get away with mischief, I had to be smarter and cover my tracks a lot better. Without a brother who approved of me, I began seeking approval from teammates and classmates routinely. I became the cool kid that knew how to get out of trouble, which was a skill very few kids my age had and I was beginning to master it. It was no longer about sharing the blame; it was about how to steal and sneak around without ever being caught. It was all I would think about. If anyone wanted to sneak into somewhere or steal something without anyone finding out, they came and got Jose.

Everyone knew I could map out the escape plan without a scratch and I wore that shit like a badge of honor.

Have you ever been the go-to person in your circle for something that needed to get done? How did it make you feel? I was the football player and the kid who got in a lot of trouble, but each time I made a mistake and got caught, I learned from those experiences and became more stealthy. This behavior solidified my ego. Everyone knew that Jose "had it", and it didn't matter how much trouble he got in, because he would return stronger and readier than ever to get back to it.

It would be modest to say I was well known--I was outright famous in middle school and even the teachers and principles knew it. If you ever sought acceptance from your peers, the first thing you discovered was who you needed to become to always be accepted. Once we have an idea of who we need to become, we become that person. I know as you read this you will understand exactly what I am referring to. I was a teenager, and it didn't matter where the approval came from so long as it came. I knew I had a responsibility to keep getting better at whatever that was. To maintain my fame, I had to be different. Everything that kids my age were doing, I would do the opposite. When kids were sagging their pants and cutting class, I was stealing from stores and feeding all my boys. What I did required more skills, courage, and degrees of difficulty and everyone knew it. Therefore the choice became easier: everyone wanted to be my friend because of what I became so quickly. I was bad, and there is no other way to put it.

Suddenly, I didn't feel so alone. I had my teammates who I played football with and a bunch of kids at school who looked up to me. The punishment and discipline at home got worse and became more routine. Although I was masterful at hiding it from my peers, my parents knew what I was becoming all too well. I was getting so good at mischief, but I made the foolish mistake of thinking that I could do the same at home. Teachers would call home, my report cards were mediocre, and I would touch stuff that wasn't mine. My stepmom would say, "idle hands are the devil's playground," and at home, the devil would use my hands however he pleased. I was too famous at school to allow being punished and grounded to stop me from being a prolific class clown and cool kid. I would get in trouble with teachers and return the next day as if it was no big deal; my classmates loved it and would follow in my footsteps. However, when they would get in trouble, their behaviors changed quickly. I knew they didn't have what it took to walk in my shoes. But too many times, those same shoes became harder to walk in because the laces were tied so tight that I knew taking them off was an impossible task. I had to own what I became. Fortunately for me, I was young, so the consequences for my actions weren't significant.

Today, I don't wear those shoes anymore, but I remember

exactly what it felt like to have them on and how much effort it took to take them off. They caused too much pain and harm over time, but instead of remaining shoeless, I decided to replace them with a better pair. This pair had the same effect on my peers, as they wanted to be around them often, but the reasons were not the same as before.

I try to live my life without falling victim to regret. Life presents us with opportunities to learn valuable lessons, and we do not choose how they come. My ego was strong--I committed my time and energy to become who I was and I owned it. My attitude became "I got this". I didn't ask for much help, and at times I still struggle with asking. My father is a very independent man, therefore he taught me the importance of being self-sufficient and knowing how to not let someone saying "no" stop me from getting what I wanted. He taught me to find a way, and that if I couldn't find a way, then the only person I should ask for help was him or my family. I value the power of independence and how it teaches the skills of adaptability and self-control.

Growing up black meant you had to be prideful, and I was culturally taught that strength and grit were the minimum requirements. Football in the inner city only enforced this type of thinking and has given me a lot of mental toughness, and for that, I express my deepest gratitude. I've learned that there are two sides to every coin and while I was strong, tough, and prideful, my ego and separation caused me to miss out on a lot of opportunities.

DO- IT -YOURSELFERS

It is important to take pride in self-sufficiency. I have learned that people are more likely to help you when you are willing to help yourself. All your life, you believed that you're capable of helping yourself, and in a lot of scenarios, you were right. You have likely created high expectations for yourself through this process. Spend enough time solving your own problems, and you will expect to solve them forever the same way. Your peers have likely watched you crushing it, solving a problem so well that you have enough in the tank to solve theirs, and they love you for it. You are on your way to major popularity and a powerful reputation for being superman. However, if you don't monitor your outputs, you will fly headfirst into disappointment and let down.

BATMAN VS. JOKER

If you are familiar with superheroes, then you know the story of Batman. Batman is by far one of the most famous and well-liked superheroes in world history. I'm certain that he may be the most loved superhero of all time because unlike all the others, he had no supernatural ability: he was just a man. Batman was a badass, he saved lives in the darkness of the night, drove cool vehicles, and fought with skills and speed. He was a wealthy man, but a simple man who committed his life to help the people of Gotham City and he was great at it. But in 2008, he encountered a villain like none other.

This villain was different, faster, smarter, and more complex. Batman was accustomed to defeating simple- minded bad guys, and it certainly led to a bump in his status and ego. In 2008, *The Dark Knight* made over $1 billion in the box office, and it was greatly due to a familiar character known as the Joker. Many of us knew from the cartoon how dangerous the Joker was, but what they did with the character in this movie was nothing short of a masterpiece. Batman was forced to face a villain that dismantled his ego, the Joker exposed Batman to the other side of his coin and it made for a thrilling story. It caused him so much disappointment that he debated whether his time as Batman was over--his pride had taken a hit and people no longer approved of him in the same way. The shoes he walked in became far too painful to walk in, and in an instant he was willing to take them off. We learned what his weakness was because someone had come along to exploit it. Once it was exposed, it led to him letting down his loved ones, his city, and most importantly, himself.

Batman remains my favorite superhero, as there is something special about his story. It takes courage to set such high expectations and live up to them over and over again, and for many years he did. With the help of very few people, he became a superhero even though he was just a normal human. I share Batman's story to remind you that as high as your expectations are and as well as you have been able to meet them, there will be a time when someone or something comes along and exposes you to the other side of your coin. Everyone has experienced what it feels like to go head to head with Joker. That voice inside your head or that gut feeling that is eating at your ego. Additionally, the Joker we battle against can be an event or circumstance as well. If the time has already come and you have faced it, I'm sure it hurt for a little while. I know you've felt like you were losing your ability to do it at a high level; people may have given up on you or no longer seem like they need your value, and that is okay.

GETTING TO KNOW YOUR EGO

You need this time to confront yourself, to learn more about who you are, and get a tight hold on your ego. Identify what you sound like, how you think, and what happens when you operate through your ego. Reflect on what opportunities you missed out on or what relationships weakened because of it. Grab a journal or something to write down a few questions in your notes.

• What areas of your life has your ego benefitted you?

• In what environments does it show the most, and why?

• When has your ego hurt yourself or others?

The answers to these questions are essential to know as this step of the process is about finally knowing when to surrender your ego. As individuals, we never truly eliminate our ego. We just don't get rid of it like it hasn't been a part of our subconscious mind the whole time. Although some may not agree with me, we need to hold onto a piece of our ego and spend a lot of time getting to know it. I refer to the ego as a separate part of us because it can be controlled and it should be.

When you were at your worst, beating up on yourself for a mistake, believe it or not, your ego helped you. Our egos keep us resilient and help restore our confidence. The most important thing is the context in which we deploy our ego, which will determine its effectiveness. I do not write this to be right, I write this to tell you the truth that we fight so hard not to believe.

Once you have taken time to understand your ego, you will spend the rest of your life practicing this step. Knowing when to surrender your ego for the betterment of your mental health and your relationship with others is an extremely important part of practicing self awareness.

Part One Summary:

Self Awareness

The journey of practicing self-awareness has never stopped for me and I don't think it ever will. As my elements change, I seem to grab hold of this practice tighter because I fear that without it, I will self-destruct. As living creatures, we possess extremely high levels of consciousness, and we need it. We are intuitive and unpredictable, which allows us to create and thrive without limits. As you continue to practice self-awareness daily, you will tap into incredible human potential. Recognizing your potential and being able to hone it and apply it to your life has allowed you to accomplish great things already. This is about having high expectations, and I know you have them. Not only have you tapped into your performance ability, you have learned ways to cultivate positive outputs consistently. Each level of achievement is directly correlated to effort, sacrifice, and execution.

As we reflect on part one, it's important that I note self-actualization is the final pillar of Maslow's Hierarchy of Needs which indicates it as the least important human necessity. While this may be true of our external possessions, it may be the most important necessity when it comes to mindset. I know that you desire more than just necessities, there is a fire inside you that wants more. The desire to become the most one can be begins with understanding who you are and how you got that way. To overcome the pain of disappointment, practicing forgiveness with yourself and others will set the stage for effective communication. Effective communication will set the standard and the expectation. You will be providing clarity to yourself and others, which is necessary to complete any critical task.

Finally, knowing when to surrender your ego so you can allow love and support in your life will be a key step going forward. It's a lesson that I learned the extremely difficult way as you will learn in later chapters. The lifelong practice of self-awareness has no instruction manual: we create our own out of necessity. We all have visions of the person we want to be in the future, and we can quite literally see that person so clearly at times. As I continue my own self- awareness journey, I remember the lessons from my teachers and mentors often. What I've learned so far is that who we become in the future is a collection of the choices made in the present.

I ask that you take this time to reflect on your life up until this point. Accept all that has transpired and display a moment of gratitude that you're alive which means your fight continues. It's now time to use everything you have learned about yourself thus far and apply it in every area of life. Embrace the process: the work begins.

MINDSET SHIFT

Chapter 5:

Comfort is Overrated

"Start where you are, with what you have.." - George Washington

Carver

We all love a success story, the story of starting from the bottom. People were counting you out and expecting you to fail; then, after years of sacrifice and hard work, you're able to achieve all the things they said you couldn't. I love those stories too. One thing we all have in common is struggle. Struggle and pain play major roles in personal growth and you know it despite sometimes not wanting to admit it. Sometimes we compete to find out who had it tougher growing up, and from what I've seen, pain and struggle certainly impacts mental toughness. In my life, I have experienced what it was like to have less, or at least feel like I did. Compared to what I saw others have, I knew that my family wasn't there, and that our situation looked nothing like what we saw in movies with happier wealthier families. Still, I was always able to eat, sleep with a roof over my head, and access to education. Most of all, I knew I was loved.

Before my brother and I moved to Queens to live full time with my dad, stepmom, and step-sister, we lived in Red Hook, Brooklyn, with Grandma Liz. Everyone knows that one older woman who everyone calls grandma even if they have no family ties to her at all--Grandma Liz was that kind of person. She had a few children of her own but they were all grown up. My dad worked full time for the NYC Housing Authority and could not take care of us full time so we stayed with grandma Liz and about 5 other kids who would become our cousins. A total of 9 of us stayed in unit 3A, a three-bedroom apartment in the Red Hook Project Buildings. The building's elevators were practically always broken, and the hallways lights flickered all day long. It wasn't the best living situation, but we all had a place to feel safe. When Grandma Liz would start cooking, it was as if the entire building came to the front door for a plate. Even people that didn't live in our building came. The news would spread so fast, the baked macaroni and collard greens wouldn't even make it out of the oven before "uncles" and "aunts" were walking in the apartment with big smiles on their faces. My brother and I were greedy kids so we knew that we had to get our plates right away, Grandma Liz always fed the younger kids first anyway. Within five minutes the food was done and all the adults were at the table gambling their money and jewelry away. For hours they smoked, laughed, and drank all night until grandma had enough and kicked everyone out until the next big gathering a few days later. Many of them worked odd jobs, hustled drugs, or didn't have any structured job at all, but back then no one judged because we all were broke. This was routine for us growing up in the projects, but it was special when adults gathered.

These occasions gave us kids the freedom to cause mischief and have fun outside while the adults were busy. We would come back after school and grandma wouldn't know that we had gotten into fights, stolen from the corner store, or hopped gates. The only thing that mattered was making sure we all made it back to 3A by dark, and if we did, grandma was happy. My two cousins Caleek and Marcus were older than us and got in a lot of trouble with the law, but they were our role models. Some nights if grandma had enough "pocket change," they would walk us to the corner store at night to grab some "midnight snacks." Everybody was allowed two bags of 25 cent chips and a 50 cent soda. That was all grandma could afford to give us so to make sure no- one asked for any we said "no eggies, no beggies, no nothing" and proceeded to cough on our cheese doodles and soda. This was how things were, it was our struggle but everyone around us was struggling too so it wasn't out of the ordinary.

Grandma Liz was in her early 60's but when it was time to give out an "ass-whooping", somehow she found strength that only a strong black woman could find. If we did something we weren't supposed to do, she would beat all of us and then we would all have to kneel on rice while facing the wall. After beating us, she was so exhausted that she would fall asleep on the couch and forget she put us in punishment. She slept with one eye open and it scared us so much that we wouldn't even try to get off our knees when she fell asleep. One time we found enough courage and tried to pull a fast one when she fell asleep and somehow we got away with it. When Grandma Liz finally woke up she came into the room and beat us again for not being there facing the wall when she opened her other eye.

Grandma Liz loved us like her own kids and we knew it. Through all of the struggling we loved her because she made having nothing not feel so bad. After all, she brought everyone together. We all either slept on the floor in the living room or on mattresses in the rooms for several years. We had little space and even fewer possessions. It was a total of nine of us living in a three-bedroom apartment and today that type of living situation is sure to create discomfort and even warrant some law enforcement attention. Back then, police came to the apartment to ask about one of our older cousins almost routinely. The combination of getting in many fights and not having much to call our own resulted in some uncomfortable moments. Fortunately, Grandma Liz had a way of making it all work out, and everyone admired her for it. Today she is 81 years old and still going strong. Every time I have gone to visit her, she'd say, "there goes my grand-baby." When she would say this, my heart would fall right out of my chest with love.

Red Hook, Brooklyn is so different now, times have changed and with time so has my perception of my upbringing. I was fortunate to have the start of my childhood I had because it taught me discomfort and how not to view it as a limitation. I'm okay with discomfort. It has taken me some time but I welcome discomfort even more now. I believe it is a sign of challenging and rewarding times ahead if I'm able to overcome it. Sometimes I fear that if I don't experience discomfort periodically, something is going wrong and I may be declining as a result. In many cases I am right.

As individuals with high expectations, when we are mentally tough enough to withstand punishment, periods of being uncomfortable doesn't knock us off our pivot. We become unstoppable. Adopt a mentality where you are comfortable being uncomfortable. If you can find the strength to do so and you're able to hold on to that amazing ability long enough without giving in, you win. Pain tolerance is a valuable variable: the person who could stand tall when life hits you with disappointment is more equipped for creating sustainable positive outputs. Comfort is overrated, and we can only experience it for so long before it begins to play with our minds. I am not encouraging a life of constant uncertainty and discomfort, but instead I'm encouraging a comfort with discomfort.

Discomfort presents us with a choice and we have the freedom to choose what we do with it.

Chapter 5 Part 2:

Find What Works

"You're already in pain, get something out of it." - Eric Thomas

Sometimes when I'm working out, I become overwhelmed with positive emotions and feel the need to scream. A lot of times I don't because I fear it would intimidate people or I would feel embarrassed, but when I'm by myself I let it out with no mercy. It's quick and just long enough for me to feel normal again. Sometimes I say things like, "I'M A BEAST", or, "I'M A F*CKING SAVAGE, I DO THIS SHIT". When I'm around a lot of people I hold these emotions in and it kills me every time. I have found that singing or rapping a melody helps the emotions ooze out undetected. Afterward, I feel great, ready to conquer the world because I just walked into discomfort and walked out with a win.

HACKING YOUR MIND

We all are aware that hackers exist, these highly skilled individuals use a computer and various forms of technology to gain unauthorized access to data. They become familiar with all the algorithms needed to generate a specific output. Furthermore, they are connected to information that, on the surface, seems impossible or restricted. I have always been fascinated by the process of hacking. It takes talent, practice, and a desire to repeatedly solve problems. It would be an insult to the human brain to call it a computer, but it certainly has some similar characteristics of a computational system. The brain uses chemicals to transmit information and the computer uses electricity: both transmit information and both have a memory that can grow. Both computational systems and our brains have evolved, requires energy to work, and can be changed and modified. Therefore, similar to how a hacker studies the technology and finds ways to gain desired outcomes, we can do the same things to our minds. Our mind becomes more powerful as we learn to direct it. Whatever outcome you, there is an algorithm that can gain access to the part of your brain than can help you achieve those results.

Unlike the computer, hacking our minds doesn't require perfect execution; it just has to work temporarily, long enough to get you through the discomfort. It wasn't long before I began practicing small techniques to quickly hack my mind in pressured moments. We can feel extremely prepared, but there are moments of resistance that are not planned for. In those moments, it's imperative that we find what works. You can buy 100 makes of the same laptop, and they will all have the most basic operating systems, but we make them unique to ourselves. The exact process happens with the human mind. We have the ability to feel emotions and experience senses. Some may not have access to all due to varying circumstances but we remain operational. Over time we learn our systems, limitations, tendencies, habits, and desires.

When we are faced with resistance, our predictable reaction is to use what we know to overcome the conflict. You mustn't freeze your operation system in these moments. Use whatever works, whatever you may have access to in that very moment, put it to use, and don't stop until it gets the job done. You are not looking for perfection here, but just enough proficiency to generate a desired outcome. When we find a way to problem solve effectively, the next time a similar issue arises, we are even more prepared because now, we have experience.

....

"Your brain is a toolbox, filled with tools you've collected over time." - Jose Duncan Jr.

....

THE TRUTH ABOUT THE BRAIN

Your brain is a toolbox filled with tools you've collected over time. Sometimes you may be missing a tool and there is no shame in borrowing someone else's and allowing them to borrow yours. A screwdriver doesn't put a nail into a wall, a hammer does, and with just one hammer you can complete hundreds of tasks. If you are going to set high expectations consistently, it's vital that you find the hammer that works for you. Self-talk became my glorified hammer. With this tool I have felt equipped to conquer discomfort wherever I am.

Repeating mantras to myself like "I can do hard things", or "I'm a beast", has allowed me to access emotional triggers that influence action. I gain access to an entirely new set of small tools. I stand in discomfort knowing that if the going gets rough again, I can pull out that hammer and start hammering away once more. Sometimes the tool will not work--maybe it's overused, dull, lacking strength needed for the job. When this happens, we tend to use it anyway because we are familiar with it and it has worked in the past. As time goes on there will be a need for better, more efficient tools because our task increases in difficulty. What is your tool?

If you haven't found your tool, have patience and begin trying out the ones that you're curious about the most. This process is difficult, and sampling through all the ways to overcome discomfort and pain can feel exhausting and perpetual. This step is about discovering your inner partner in crime, and to find that person, you must keep searching despite occasionally finding nothing. Remain diligent, because in time, I promise that person will appear because you will have no other choice. Finding what works is a valuable step for those who value their performance: the outcome is very important but not more than the process.

Focusing on big goals isn't enough to keep you determined and motivated when resistance arises. Pursuing small goals along the way creates the momentum needed to not give up on ourselves. Momentum is generated by small victories, therefore to win your battle, you will need to have a lot of small wins. I am all about the small victories. The focus, courage, and discipline needed is so profound because discomfort has no preset magnitude. The conflict can be big or small, but how we respond to it does not have to fluctuate. Develop an understanding of what works and what doesn't, and do what works over and over again.

In Division 1 football, every team you play has talent, and talent is certainly not the deciding factor--although it helps a lot. The team that has discipline, cohesiveness, and talent will have a greater chance of beating an opponent without those team traits. In football, there are so many unexpected occurrences that can arise and it can be impossible to determine which player or play will directly impact the outcome of the competition. To win the game, each player has to do their job which is to win small battles with the opponent. There are hundreds of small wins and losses throughout the game, but the players who can win the most critical and impactful battles give their team the best chances of winning. No one knows when that moment would occur before starting the game, but we know it will happen. This is why I love team sports, particularly football. I learned that every member of the team deals with small discomforts over and over again so that everyone can win. It's bigger than any individual player.

MENTAL GAME-PLANING

Performers expect to win, prepare to win, and play to win, and this is a non-negotiable fact. Each week during the college seasons, Coach Fleming and the other assistant coaches would draw up a game plan for our next opponent. We had a losing culture but the determination to go out and compete again to win never wavered. The coaches would spend hours in the coordination room talking, writing on a whiteboard, and thinking of a way to put guys in the best position to win their battles. As a captain of the team sometimes I would visit the coach's offices and sit in on these meetings for some time and in those moments I felt like I had a bigger role in the outcome of the game. One day I walked in the coaches' meeting to ask my position coach if we could watch game film. Instead, my defensive coordinator told me to come in and watch it with the entire staff. That day we watched a tape of the University of New Hampshire Wildcats. Historically, they were a good team with decent talent but played disciplined, smart football. They were the only organization in our conference that experienced 8 consecutive playoff berths. We hadn't been able to beat them during my time there, so as a senior I was determined.

I looked around the room only to see empty cups of coffee, a game-plan binder, used up markers, and stacks play sheets on the table. It became clear to me that the coaches spent their entire Sunday afternoon in this room together. That day they explained the game plan on each side of the ball, the goal of the defense, and objective for the offense. Within those large goals, they explained the position group goals and objectives, but they would not stop there. It wasn't common to speak about individual objectives amongst the entire staff; instead, the positional coach was assigned with that task. That week in practice we were given our task and taught why it was important to do our jobs as it affected the rest of the team. After Friday afternoon, after all the technical work was complete and the game-plan was understood, the next 24 hours were designated to the most important variable, mental preparation. Although all week we were expected to be mentally preparing, everyone knew that the 24 hours before game-time required a concentrated approach to our mental focus. The coaches were never in charge of how we showed up on Saturday morning and we all were college athletes--we took ownership of that.

FIND YOUR THING, WHATEVER THAT IS

My defensive coordinator had this saying he would often say the night before at the team dinner: "do what you need to do to get yourself ready to play men". The output was showing up ready to play, and it was our job to be ready when the whistle blew for kickoff. It didn't matter if you needed to study your plays all night, play video games, go for a walk, chill with your friends, or stay up to 4 am. As long as you did your job to the best of your ability when it came time to compete, no one questioned it. In the locker room before team sports you will likely notice dozens of rituals and amongst those were music playing, stretching, cleaning, and watching tv. Bible reading was amongst the popular ones in my locker room--a lot of my teammates had a spiritual approach to their preparation and I admired that. Before we bonded as a team, we expected everyone to enjoy loud music to prepare, but as time went on we would lower the music out of respect for teammates who enjoyed other forms of mental preparation. I was the video watcher and cleaner. I would try to organize everything in my lockers to steady my mind.

I knew that once I stepped on the field, my adrenaline would be through the roof so I needed to spend the few hours before the game calming myself down. I watched motivational voice-overs and speeches to feel empowered. Each week was the same, and if my ritual was thrown off, I felt thrown off, so it took a lot of practice to repeat this routine whether the game was home or away. I felt that preparing this way gave me the best chance to perform at my best and achieve the output I was hoping for. Winning or losing the game didn't alter my rituals, the only thing that could alter them was if I wasn't prepared to do my best and this didn't happen very often. This was my senior year. It took me years to perfect it. There were a lot of failed attempts along the way. Loud music didn't work for me, it only distracted me more. Reading certainly wasn't my thing yet, and I didn't know what to pray for. It was something about arriving on gameday and reorganizing my locker while listening to Eric Thomas motivational videos that did it for me. I found what worked and I utilized it, I believed in it, and I made it unique for me. Life has become the same game for me, and today I am always finding new habits and rituals that serve me and my greater purpose.

Experiencing discomfort and resistance does cause disappointment and always will if we allow it. The discomfort may last a lot longer than you anticipated, but in those moments we are faced with two options: find a way to overcome and do our best or decide to do nothing and hope for the best.

We don't do HOPE. We have built such high expectations for our performance so we shouldn't hope for anything. Instead, we expect it and take actions to influence the desired outcome. When faced with these difficult decisions I believe it's critical that we take some time to discover what works for us, as long as we intend to do our best. Our actions need to reflect our desires, and there is no shame if we need to go into dark places to pull something out of you.

···

Whatever you think you need, you already have in you to get started.

···

We have tools in our toolbox for the struggles of life: use them fearlessly and often. There are many books, videos, articles, and coaches that can teach you the use of different tools to find your way. Be willing to surrender your ego, and welcome the help when it's made available to you. If it takes more than one tool, so be it. I encourage you to use the entire toolbox itself if you must, but it's up to you to find what works. Generating consistent positive outcomes is not an easy task, but we don't do EASY.

Chapter 6:

The Ultimate Superpower

"Consistency is key" - Every successful person I meet today

I've always been the youngest out of all my cousins growing up. When they would get permission to go outside to play, Grandma Liz made sure they took her grand-baby Jose with them. Kids my age and younger always hung out with me and actually looked up to me. Somehow, when I was around my older brother and cousins I was the annoying one that no one wanted the responsibility of watching. I spent a lot of time with Grandma and her sisters in the apartment because I didn't want anyone to feel like they needed to babysit me. Therefore it was common to find me sitting on the floor of a tight 3 bedroom apartment, biting my nails and watching my grandmothers doze off. Grandma was always falling to sleep on the sofa with the TV on Family Feud and her cat Black Beauty searching around the living room for dropped food. One day I decided to go outside to hang out with everyone in the park right outside of our project complex. Everyone was outside, the sprinklers were on, and the adults sat on the benches talking and smoking cigarettes. Project complexes in NYC all looked the same and it was very common that areas with grass were lined by black metal gates about 3 feet tall. I was 8 years old and stood just a bit taller than 3 feet. Back then, everyone claimed they were athletes and sometimes a normal day playing outside turned into intense competitions. To show off your athletic ability in the projects you had to run and hop the 3ft gate without using hands. All my cousins could do it because they were all 10 years old or older. As simple as it seems today, back then this was an accomplishment that earned you the right to hang out with the cool kids on the block. The adults on the benches always yelled at them when they were hopping gates because occasionally someone would not make it over clean and fall.

"Stop hopping them damn gates!" My aunt Neicy would call out. We all respected Aunty but not enough to stop doing the only activity that confirmed if you were an athlete or not.

My cousin Caleek was the best. He was a little older than me but he would clear the gate with about a whole foot length of height. We all looked up to him. He was the ultimate athlete. He was skinny, but his limbs were long and it was as if he wasn't afraid of hurting himself. His parkour skills were unmatched by anyone else in the neighborhood. In the projects you were likely to find some of the best raw athletes you've ever seen in your life. Kids would do backflips, aerials, pikes, and tucks by the time they were only 11 years old.

No one took gymnastic lessons; most families couldn't afford to send their kids to professional coaches. The talent we had came from spending all day outside trying to show off how athletic we were. We would spend entire days outside with little food or water. When I went outside that day, everyone was taking turns hopping the gates, and Caleek was leading the way. I went to join them, though everyone knew that I still needed to use my hands to hop the gates. Although everyone started this way, they made fun of me every day for it. I joined them and decided to hop the gates with my hands and be cool, but I got no attention for it. Deep down I felt like I was capable of hopping without hands but the thought of falling on my face frightened me. As a kid I always had the fear of breaking my neck or hurting myself so badly that I could never recover from it, and this fear kept me from escaping an average belief about myself. I had high expectations for my athletic ability, but had below-average courage and I could not shake it.

ONE OF THE TOUGHEST DAYS

My cousin Caleek called me over to show me how to hop the gate with no hands. All the kids were watching me and I enjoyed the attention. He explained what I needed to do. He was a wizard and deserved a gold medal if there was a Project Olympics. He took a few steps back, ran to the gate, and hopped it. After he came back, he said, "See how I did that? You gotta get a running start."

So I tried. In that moment as I was backing up preparing to try and conquer my fear, I had not yet realized that this was going to be one of the toughest days of my childhood. I ran to the gates and when I got to about one foot from it, I stopped, grabbed it, and hopped over. All my cousins laughed at me. I felt frightened and I would try again, but still, I grabbed the gate first. Every time I would chicken out, Caleek would go and jump it to show me how simple it was. If only he knew that to me this was the scariest thing I had ever attempted he might have left me alone to grab and hop the gate until I was older, taller, and braver. I would try again and again but now instead of grabbing the gate I would just come to a complete stop. All my cousins would continue laughing and hopping the gates to show me how easy it was and it was beginning to hurt my feelings.

I started crying and getting angry and I wanted to fight my cousin Renee because she laughed the loudest and always picked on me. She was a girl and she couldn't hop the gate but no one expected her to, and I hated her for it. We had been outside for an hour now and the rubber under the sneakers that I shared with my brother began coming off and tearing at the front. Growing up, when we saw a kid with this, we made fun of them; we would say that their "sneakers were talking." If you got holes under your sneakers everyone knew you spent a lot of time at the park because in the summertime, the concrete would burn right through them in a matter of weeks. After about an hour, I built up enough courage to jump and I paid the price for it. As I jumped, I came down on the gate and my leg slid down as the gates peeled the skin off my right shin. Now I had blood dripping down onto my sneakers, but I finally got some attention from my cousins. Caleek was getting frustrated with me so he showed me one more time: there was a key piece to hopping the gate that I noticed I was missing at that moment. Caleek would run to the gate and before he jumped his hands would go back and he would turn his body sideways before he tucked his knees. My other cousins did it too, but Caleek did the jump so well it was easier to see the change in his body position.

After he completed his jump I tried again, but the blood running down my leg created so much fear. I wasn't prepared for another bruise. Caleek left me at the gate and when he did, so did everyone else, even my brother. I was left there alone, it was getting darker outside, and I hadn't eaten a meal since the morning. It was normal that once we were outside, food choices became ice cream from the truck, a beef patty with cheese, or frozen icy's until grandma ordered or cooked dinner. The blood on my leg had dried and my legs were tired. I knew that if I left the gate that day to go play with the others, all the tears and time spent would mean nothing. I was sure that I wouldn't get the same attention the next time I tried, so I stayed. The only benefit now was that I would focus on what Caleek showed me without fear of being embarrassed. What are you willing to fail at if you didn't fear embarrassment? If other opinions no longer mattered to you, will you keep trying?

I walked back and made a few more attempts at hopping the gate. I had tried so many times and no longer needed to grab the gate but I still couldn't make it over. I would jump on top of the gate but fall back down to the ground. Something wasn't right. My cousins always said that "if you can get on top of the gate, you can get over." He believed that once you're able to get the right height, the most challenging part was done. I thought that I didn't have enough running space so I tried that, and got the same results. By this time I was consistently making it on top of the gate, so I decided to climb on top of the gate and jump off onto the grass a few times to see what it felt like to land on the other side. After doing this a few times I realized that I was landing on both feet, and Caleek never landed on both feet at the same time. So I jumped off and took another attempt and cleared the gate. The first true sign of progress was made when I cleared the gate with my front foot, but my back foot didn't because my shoelaces got caught in the gate and I fell on the grass. By this point I had fallen so many times it no longer bothered me. The only positive was that I made it over the gate despite not landing on my feet. I finally jumped and ended up on the other side, which was an accomplishment in itself. I knew what I needed to do now. After dozens of failed attempts I gained clarity.

The sprinklers went off and the adults began packing their things to go inside for the night and all my cousins were being called in, so I knew that I had to go inside soon and I desperately wanted to clear the gate that night. I tried a few more times with all the right techniques. I tucked my back foot as my body turned to hop the gate but I still didn't clear it, only this time I landed onto the gate and fell off onto the grass instead of backward. That night I wasn't able to clear the gate but I knew I made a lot of progress even though no one was there to see it. My sneakers were completely torn at the bottom and my mouth was very dry--I was exhausted.

The next day before everyone went outside to play, I snuck out of the apartment to go try jumping the gate again. I could barely sleep because I was imagining what it felt like to make it over without falling. Have you ever been so anxious about something that you could hardly get any sleep? If you have, then you would understand what I was feeling and how important doing this was to me. I was rested and my legs were fresh. I was confident and had no fear of hurting myself. I ran back, ran forward, tucked my leg, turned my body sideways, jumped off my right leg, tucked my feet, cleared the gate, and landed on the grass with my left foot then my right. FINALLY!! I cleared it, I hopped my first gate, I looked around to see if anyone saw me. No one did, but I was still happy. I began wondering why I feared that the whole time. I could understand it--it felt so simple, it felt like that was what I was supposed to be doing the entire time at my height. I was so excited that when everyone came outside later I called Caleek and showed him that I could clear the gate now. All my cousins came over and it made me nervous. So I ran back, ran forward, tucked my leg, turned my body sideways, jumped off my right leg, tucked my feet, cleared the gate, and landed on the grass with my left foot then my right.

Everyone started yelling, "Oh." I was so excited as I stood there on the grass, looking back at them. I am smiling now, just writing about it. Caleek gave me a hug and even Renee was happy for me. A few of my cousins were shocked because the last time they saw me at the gate I was bleeding from my leg and crying about not making it over. What they didn't know was that I stayed at that gate for three more hours trying over and over again. When they went to play at the sprinkler I was still at the gate with a dry mouth and talking sneakers trying to conquer my fear. They missed how I finally made it to the top of the gate, they missed my laces getting caught in the gate and falling, they missed me climbing on the gate and hopping off, all they saw now was me clearing the gate repeatedly. We all spent that afternoon hopping gates together and watching Caleek do flips off the gates. It was one of the happiest days I had in the RedHook projects. That day I learned that even the people who know and love you the most will not always believe you can accomplish great achievements, but it's not their fault. It was up to me to give them a reason to respect my determination. When I finally did generate a basis for validation, it wouldn't matter if they believed or not.

STAND IN DISCOMFORT LONG ENOUGH

Growing up, I have relied heavily on my ability to withstand discomfort and punishment in hopes that I would become better as a result. Sometimes I question why I wouldn't quit and consider that I may have issues with detaching. Today I can admit that I do struggle with detachment, and it has been the price I've paid for refusing to quit or give up once I decide to start anything. My expectations have risen so high that pressure moments no longer bother me. I believe that if I can keep getting up after I get knocked down that at some point, the knockdowns would no longer affect me. Instead of having a clear vision of what I wanted to accomplish to fuel my drive, I would keep pushing blindly without direction which led to experiencing disappointment almost routinely.

Have you had moments in your life where you refused to quit but in the back of your mind you didn't know why? This was the feeling I had about every challenge in my life. It wasn't always supported by a desire to win, but instead by the fear of being called a quitter. As I reflect, some things I held onto for way too long, and others I held onto just long enough to make a breakthrough. True perseverance must be deeply rooted in our upbringing; there is no switch to turn it on and off. To be known as someone who isn't a quitter is the most important character trait I possess and the most proudest of.

. . . .

There is power in repetition, and with enough practice, you can hone this skill and use it as a superpower.

. . . .

Some individuals are blessed with superior talent and talent should never be discounted or denied. Honing the superpower of repetitions will create a strong argument that you possess superior talent as well. "Nothing great is ever accomplished without practice and overcoming failure," said in some form by every happily successful person I connect with today. As much as I wanted to believe something else, life always reminds me of this timeless fact. To gain anything significant or learn a valuable skill, it's required that you sacrifice time. Time is the only variable that cannot be manipulated. There is no getting around it and this can be extremely aggravating. With every minute you sacrifice, you need to believe in what the sacrificed time rewards you down the line. Repetition is the reoccurrence of an action or event. Therefore, there isn't much that needs to be changed or done differently but instead just done repeatedly. Repetition is NOT a step in your process, but instead, it will become one of the most important guiding principles in your life. Proper preparation has a direct impact on our performance, and preparation takes reps.

The repetition superpower is just reinforcement. As humans, we can forget that this superpower is always available, but life has a funny way of reinforcing it again. That funny way is losing, it's failing at the thing that is important to you. Failing and losing repeatedly is disappointing and can certainly take a toll on the ego, but what you gain is perspective. We get to a point where the disappointment is so painful that we reflect on what it was like to win and be happy. We reflect on what actions we took and how we were able to make the initial breakthrough. Finally, we assess what has changed since. At that moment we realize that we stopped reinforcing behaviors that allowed us to be at our best, and know that we must practice those behaviors again. Winning and losing are not the direct result of how many reps you put in; sacrificing all your time to learn or achieve something will not guarantee you will reap the reward.

Repetition only guarantees that you will get better, it guarantees that you give yourself a better chance at getting whatever it is you want, and most of all it shows you care. I have never believed I was talented, so I decided that in order to compete amongst others who were, I needed to work that much harder. Don't lower your expectations because things aren't going well and you're experiencing disappointment at every turn--instead, increase your reps. It may feel unfair that you need to sacrifice more of your time to have a chance at the things other people have achieved, but if you want what you say you want, then there is no other way. Be careful of shortcuts, limit comparing yourself to others, and just keep showing up for yourself.

There is a term we use as health & fitness coaches called motor learning. This form of learning creates a permanent change in our ability to execute a motor skill as a result of practice and experience. Along with motor learning is muscle memory, which is the ability to convert a motor task into memory through repetition. These terms will determine how well you can perform a task. They require time and sacrifice, and although everyone has access to practice them, many aren't willing to withstand the failures that come with them. After all, we are talking about superpowers, and superpowers like these come with a price.

Today, if I ever see a 3-foot gate, I relive that moment as a kid all over again. I imagine taking a few steps back, I begin running at the gate, and when I get close enough, I turn my body sideways, push off my right foot, and tuck my left foot. I would see myself clearing the gate and landing on the other side, one foot at a time. I'd look back at the gate and remember that kid with holes under his shoes and blood running down his leg that refused to quit, and in those moments, I thank him.

To the person who feels like they're running in place making no progress, I will like to encourage you.

••

Don't give up on yourself. If you cannot find the courage to believe in YOU, then no one will.

••

Chapter 7:

Next Play

"Dust yourself off, and try again" - Aaliyah (Singer, Songwriter)

In the game of football, there are very few moments that you know will greatly impact the outcome of the game. I've told you before that winning and losing comes down to how well each player executes their own battles throughout the game. Although momentum will favor both sides at different points of the contest, there can be some moments where the shift in momentum knocks you off your feet, and as a team, you feel like you can't get back up. As a player, you prepared all week. You studied your opponent so extensively to ensure you don't make the mistake of causing the heaviest momentum shift. When I was on the field with my brothers, I knew regardless if one of us made that critical mistake we would all need to continue fighting. We all had the responsibility of righting each other's wrongs by increasing our focus and efforts in the goal to take back momentum. But, when the increased level of focus and effort did not create the impact needed, everyone felt guilty and careless for making a mistake because we all knew one important thing. Hadn't the player made the critical mistake, the outcome may have been entirely different. As a result, the team's morale would have been better and everyone would still compete with confidence.

THE FIRST START

On October 18, 2014, I made my first start as a collegiate football player against The University of Richmond in Richmond, Virginia. I had never been to Virginia and I wasn't prepared for how hot the weather was in October. As for the Richmond players, 87 degrees in October was just another day. The sun engulfed the entire field, and the water jugs could barely stay cool throughout warmups. "Joe, Jose Duncan is going to start this game at defensive-end," said my defense coordinator Coach Rektis in the pregame locker room. Coach Rektis was a man I looked up to in many ways and Coach Cogniglio who he called Joe was one of the best coaches I ever had in my life.

From across the locker-room, Coach Joe gestured for me to come to him. When I walked over to him he told me in the calmest voice, "you're going out with the first-team defense today." The moment he said it I looked around the locker room and all the freshmen who had traveled were smiling. They knew what that brief exchange meant and I've been working hard all season to earn the coaches' trust so I could hear those words.

Deep down I knew Coach Cogniglio was not comfortable with me starting as a freshman, but sitting at 0-7 on the season with no playoff chances, Coach Rektis thought it was time to do some grooming of his future players.

My nerves on the sideline went crazy before the game, I didn't know how to pregame warmup for my first start, I debated between playing it cool like I've been here before or exhaust myself out by over practicing my techniques. I chose to "over practice" my techniques. I was the only true freshman on the field and I knew the coaches expected me to be a producing member of the 2014 Rhode Island defense. I desperately wanted to be, however, the high expectations made me nervous. It was the 8th game of the season and we had yet to capture our first win. I'd earned playing time throughout the season, but I was never asked to play a starting role until now. Starting roles meant that you took on a larger percentage of the success or failure of your team's performance. Everyone wanted to be the starter but when things weren't going so well, it was not so fulfilling.

When the game began, my team started the game on offense, this gave me time to ponder my responsibilities on the sideline, I knew the game plan on defense but wasn't quite sure I had enough experience or talent to execute it. It was too late for that now as I found myself running out on the field with the first-team defense. I knew that me running out the field meant I took someone's job. I replaced a player who previously held this position because the coaching staff felt I could do a better job. That is the reality of team sports, as much as you love your teammates and respect them, it's still a competition, and you're either fighting to earn playing time or keeping a freshman like me from taking your job. Being supported by 10 other guys on defense felt like it wasn't enough for me. I felt as if I was alone on the field. I feared that if I made a mistake, there was no one coming to have my back.

Have you ever felt like you knew exactly what to do in life, but when all the pressure and expectations settle in, you completely forget everything you know? I knew my responsibilities and performed them well in practice that week, but somehow a plane ride to Virginia created the perfect scenario for me to feel like I knew nothing at all. With my hand in the turf in my 3 point stance, I looked across the line and locked eyes with a 6'7" offensive tackle with massive hands and feet. I was certain that he required custom made cleats and gloves because I had never seen shoes his size in stores. From the scouting report, I knew he was about 315 pounds and one of their best players. Throughout my entire college career, I would look across at these caliber players every week and figure out how I was going to measure up. At that moment we locked eyes and I knew there was no turning back, I had to just do what I have done my whole life. I had to remind myself to just have fun playing the game I loved, and do it with effort and energy. I've never felt like I had any actual talent, but my effort had gotten me to my first start at a division 1 college. It was "GO TIME" now and I wasn't going to abandon what I knew best.

The game began, I ran around battling and threw my body all over the place to help my teammates make plays. I held my own with this 300lbs guy and it felt empowering. He would try to grab the back of my jersey with his huge hands to move me out of my position. Many times he was somewhat successful, other times I gave him hell, but if you saw him today he might tell the story differently.

If you played defensive for Coach Rektis, it was understood that everyone had a job: everyone was responsible for holding their positions. The expectation was that if you couldn't do it standing on two feet, you threw your body instead. Up until that moment, I had played in hundreds of football games, and I was very familiar with playing defensive and how each position played a key role in the team's overall performance. I settled in quickly, the nerves went away, and I began to raise my own expectations during the game. Being a part of the starting defensive at URI was the reason

I signed my scholarship. This was what I was supposed to be doing. As for the upperclassman defensive end that held the position before me, we both knew this was now my job. I finished that game with six tackles, two tackles for loss, and my first two career sacks. For my first-ever start in college, that was very impressive and I knew it. However, we would go to 0-8 on the season as we lost the game 37-0. When the score was 17-0 and we still had a chance, I made one of those critical mistakes that I've referenced before. It was the kind of mistake that Coach Cogniglio knew before the game a freshman defensive lineman could make on his first start. I broke the first rule of playing team sports, DO YOUR JOB!

It was a pressure moment and all week we prepared for a moment like it and I knew my job. I knew exactly where I needed to be and why I was asked to be there. Somehow the pressure of the moment created uncertainty, doubt, and a lack of discipline altogether. There are those moments in life where you are doing everything right and executing at a high level but a moment arises where the pressure is so high that you go against everything you know. When this happens, it invites the average to sneak back into our lives. I was about to have my moment, and it shifted the momentum so much that I felt we never recovered as a defense during the remainder of the game.

It was 4th down and 1 yard to go for Richmond and we had them back up on their 5 yard line. This meant that if we were successful at stopping them, it could set up our offense in a great position to score and shift the momentum back in our favor. In practice, Coach asked me to hold the C gap all game. The C gap was the most ran in opening in modern-day football because it gave the ball carrier the best opportunity to get outside and break a long run. I also knew that previous game plans called for me to be in the B gap, but for this team, it was critical that I stayed in the C gap. I knew where I needed to be but somehow my doubt influenced me to be elsewhere. Up until that point I already had made a bunch of plays and showed Coach Rektis why it was a great idea to give me a shot with the first team. The play began, and the running back took the ball and ran right through the opening that I left vacant before the play began, and what happened next felt like a punch in the gut.

The Richmond running back bounced outside, and within seconds the entire defense was chasing him down the field trying to prevent him from scoring. I was sprinting as fast as I could but wasn't making up any ground. I knew at that moment that I had messed up, and I was certain that my entire team would hate me for allowing this to happen at such a critical moment.

My legs began to feel heavy and the air from my lungs felt dry. I wasn't catching this guy, I had no chance. Nothing is worse than making a mistake and knowing that you can't fix it on your own. You are incapable of redoing it, and now you must live with the results. After about 50 yards, our starting middle linebacker and NFL prospect Andrew Bose was able to catch up to the ball carrier and bring him down.

Everyone called him Bose. He was a gifted football player who commanded the defense. He was also my host during my official visit and one of the biggest reasons I committed to play at the URI.

When Bose caught up to him and pulled him to the ground, the pain in my chest went away. The 3 long seconds of anxiety I felt seemed to fade away and I knew that despite my mistake, we had a chance. We could play the next play. On that drive, we stopped Richmond from scoring and it turned out that my coaches forgave me for my mistake because I kept playing. The very next play, I felt I had made up for my mistake. I did a speed rush off the ball, did a tight swim move and I was able to get around that 315lb mammoth of a man to get a sack. I even made the quarterback fumble the football. All 22 players on the field were scrambling to gain possession of the football, and amidst all the scrambling, Derrick Holmes, the other freshman on the field recovered the football.

Momentum had finally shifted in our favor, but the time on the clock expired soon after and we would not be able to capitalize.

We returned in the second half, but it felt like as a team we were never able to overcome the disappointment of being outplayed so often. I couldn't help but feel that I was a part of the problem, I desperately wanted to be a part of the solution.

After the game, sitting on the bus with 50 other disappointed teammates, I felt hopeless. I had one of the best football games in my life while making a critical mistake. Up until that point I had never played so many plays during a game. I played the whole game except for a few substitutions to catch my breath. I didn't want to come out, and the score continued to rise in Richmond's favor, but I just wanted to keep playing. I was having fun. This was what football was all about. As hopeless as I felt, I still knew that I had accomplished something great.

I learned a valuable lesson as a freshman football player on October 18, 2014 in Richmond, Virginia. The lesson was that no matter what happens to you or around you, you must play the next play. I learned how important it is to keep playing the game. At any moment, the momentum could shift back in our favor and put us in the position to get ahead. Next play mentality became my standard as a player, and it has impacted my life outside of football as well. Whether you're winning by 40 or losing by 40 it's important that you keep playing. Check the statistics in the end. Looking back to see who's catching you will only slow you down. When you sacrifice time, money, and resources to increase your chances of winning, and you lose instead, know that the next decision you make is an important one. No person can control the output. Instead, we focus our efforts on the input with the expectation that it will pay off.

Next play mentality became next quarter, next game, next class, next project, next conversation, and next location. I try to not dwell on the outcome and consistently remind myself that my best work is yet to come. How do we know when we are at our best? We form that judgment based on our past actions, but even that is a matter of perspective.

• •

If you have another shot at it, then make that next one your best.

• •

The shot you previously completed may become your best over time, but you will not find out if you stop.

WHAT HAVE YOU DONE FOR ME LATELY?

"What have you done for me lately?" was a saying my coaches in college used often as it related to the players' production. Back then, it felt like they lacked gratitude, as if they were never satisfied with us as players. Since then, I've grown a liking to the saying and even say it to my clients today. It has become a reminder that how we show up each day is of utmost importance. Whether we are motivated or not, showing up for the next opportunity lets others know they can trust us and count on us when we are needed.

What have you done for you lately? Are you practicing the necessary behaviors that give you the best opportunity to keep playing? How consistent is your work ethic? You'll need to ask yourself the difficult questions because the majority of us are fighting our insecurities. We aren't going to ask you the most difficult questions because we realize we are simultaneously asking ourselves. The accountability is yours to bear; it will be more favorable this way. Find the answers to the challenging questions and keep progressing.

MAKE THE ADJUSTMENT

Adapt the next play mentality in every aspect of your life; you will notice some significant benefits right away. The first change you are likely to see is that you judge yourself a lot less. You begin reflecting on your preparation without tearing yourself down. You will likely grow an acceptance of the problems, and you will now focus your energy on solutions.

To follow, your preparation will improve greatly as you seek to make the adjustments needed from your previous outputs. With that combination, you are likely to save the most valuable currency in the world: TIME. Next play mentality increases action and execution while decreasing over-thinking and procrastination.

Keep getting up when you get knocked down, get back into the game because your future self is relying on the current you to keep playing.

Chapter 8:

Know Where Your Help Is

"Know where your help is.." - Pete Rektis (Football Coach)

The game of football raised me, the game of football made me who I am, the game of football saved my life. In sports and life, when your coach or a leader speaks, it's vital that you listen critically. Growing up as athletes, we were spoken to a lot more than the average kids our age. However, if you've been part of any team before, it's likely that you've sat and listened to coaches, leaders, and mentors speak. During these events, the speaker would say something that resonates with the players, which invited us to think deeper. We may not have understood the topic's depth because we hadn't gained enough experience in life about what they were referring to. Yet, those statements stick with us, and we carry the thought of those powerful messages everywhere we go until we find ourselves in circumstances where they become relevant. Sometimes, a saying as simple as "life is short" is very clear and easily understood.

However, we truly grasp the depth of the saying when we lose someone we love. When the loved one is young, the death is tragic, or caused by health complications, we perceive the passing as early or sudden. For a period of time we commit ourselves to change, our caution levels are raised, we improve our health, and we follow through on our goals with the memory of the person in mind. We do that because there is no doubt in our minds that life has many uncertainties, and that fear of death drives us into action.

Then, there are things that we do know, things that we all have experienced in our lives. Our parents taught us some important lessons and we begin experiencing circumstances that bring relevance to the lessons right away. Through trial and error, fall and rise, and self exploration, we form an understanding of basic vital life lessons. Life goes on, we grow and connect, and some lessons steadily remain and the depth of its meaning grows because we have seen patterns of the same behaviors.

DO YOUR JOB!

I've valued being on a team my whole life. I believe that everyone needs some type of team, as there are things we all miss and could use the support of others to figure out. On the field you play with ten other guys, and each player has their own individual job within the overall structure. I've spoken about the saying "DO YOUR JOB" in the previous chapter because it's the most important statement in organizations that rely on individuals to produce collectively. When I got to college, I had been playing organized team football for 11 years already. In those 11 years, I not only knew the importance of doing my job but I knew the job of everyone on the field and why the execution of their jobs was so important for the outcome of the game. In both youth and high school football, my coaches made me play both sides of the ball, and for many years I was even a kicker. I could talk football with anyone, I knew the game, the game is all I ever knew. I understood it in such depth that it was hard to lose an argument about the technicality of it with anyone.

As one of eleven, I always knew my teammates had my back, and I theirs. No mistake of one person was too great that ten others guys couldn't make up for, and this was the beauty of the game. My freshman year of college I earned a lot of playing time. Those opportunities to play so early benefited me greatly. The expectations were low but the optimism about my potential from coaches was very obvious. This meant that I had raw ability and football knowledge, but it also meant that I was going to make a lot of mistakes. Unlike high school, I truly had one job and my effort determined whether I watched or played the game. With dreams of playing in the NFL, I knew watching from the sidelines was certainly out of the question, so I earned playing time right away.

Rhode Island brought me in to play defensive end, which meant my job was to be the first line of defensive on the outer edges of a football formation. As stated before, in Coach Rektis's defense, everyone had a job, and if the game- plan required you to protect the edge of the defense, it was in your best interest that you did. Sometimes having a great understanding about football and confidence in my athletic ability led to going off script at times to make plays. When it worked and I made the nice play, everyone slapped my helmet and showered me with "that-a boy's". When I free- styled and made a critical mistake, the coaches pulled me out of the game, replaced me, and the team was forced to make up for my lack of consideration of everyone's effort.

It's safe to say I free-styled often. At the time, I had been strapping up my cleats for twelve years and that experience gave me the confidence needed to make plays, and let's make no mistake about it, I did. But this was different, everyone had been playing just as long and didn't care that I thought I knew best. During the fourth quarter of an important conference game, I decided to freestyle. I'd done this many times and I knew it worked. I would take a fake step inside and come back outside. This move worked all my life and I was determined to keep perfecting it. The play began and I took two jabbed steps inside to fake out the offensive lineman and on my third step I took a hard step to the right, to complete the move I ended with an arm over swim move. The ball carrier was now in my sight and I was right where I needed to be to make the play. I knew that if he took one more step outside, my freestyle would once again prove effective.

Instead, he took a hard jab step with his left foot and cut back into the inside and picked up about 15 yards. 15 yards gained meant a new set of downs and more time off the clock. This was bad news for my team. After the play, Coach Rektis called me to the sideline and replaced me, so there I went jogging off the field trying to not make eye contact with him because I knew what he was going to tell me and I didn't like it. I tried to create separation between him and me by walking to the other end. He continued to ask for me and tell coaches to find me and get me to him right away. I didn't want to be told I made a mistake--that was clear and I didn't understand why I needed to be reminded of it.

"Couldn't he just let it go and get back to coaching the game and not complaining about me?" I thought. When I finally made my way over to him, he noticed I was upset. My body language made it very clear that I didn't care what he had to say. Coach Rektis removed one side of his coaching headset and proceeded to take off his sunglasses, which he did often during the game. Everyone knew it was his way of calming himself down before speaking. When his sunglasses were on and the headset was pressed to his head, he would break out into full pissed off coach mode, yelling and talking with an extremely stern voice. Therefore, when I noticed this wasn't his reaction I felt a little more at ease. He wrapped his arm around my shoulders and brought me into his personal space, looked me right in the eyes, and asked me, "what did you see?"

I felt confused. He was giving me the opportunity to justify my mistake, and for a moment I felt like he trusted me as much as I trusted my freestyle pass rush moves. I thought for a moment: I knew this was a test, and I knew that how I answered this question would shape his perception of me as a player. I answered, "I thought I could make the play coach." He said nothing for a moment and took a glance back at the field. He finally looked back at me and said, "You should've made that play, next time you will make that play."

I stood there in complete shock because I had never been coached in that way after making a selfish mistake. I thought that was all he needed to tell me before I went back in. To my surprise, he never put me back in that game, and I watched the remainder of the fourth quarter on the sideline. He demanded that I do it right next to him. Instead of using that as discipline, he took those moments to teach me important lessons about the game of football that I thought I already knew. He began pointing out different players on separate plays, mostly veteran players who've been playing college football longer than I have. He pointed out how they did their jobs and why it was important, he explained what would happen if they decided to do their own thing like I did. He explained how their choices on each play impacted the structure of his defense.

He kept repeating a familiar statement that game. I've heard him say it to other players in practice and meetings, but it was my turn to learn the depth of its meaning. It was my turn to learn the meaning--it always made sense when he said it, but somehow on that day I knew exactly what it meant for me. The statement was so profound that I can never forget it, and it's one of the statements that I hold very near my heart. Anytime I get an opportunity to share it with others, I do not hesitate. The statement he kept repeating was, *"Know where your help is."*

Coach Rektis reminded me that everyone on the field had a job and in the case that one of us didn't do our job, there was a structure in place to make up for it. He reminded me that I had outside help, so instead of making a move inside to go out, I could have made a move outside to go in. Knowing where your help is meant recognizing when there wasn't any help. I didn't know where my help was during the play, so I needed to execute my responsibilities. Coach also let me know that before making important decisions that could jeopardize others, it was important that I communicated with them. He believed that if I could at least let them know my intentions before the play, if things went wrong, they knew I may need help.

I sat out the rest of that game because I needed to; there are consequences for making selfish decisions. My confidence and ambition had been empowering and had led to achieving great milestones. As the achievements grew, so did my ego. However, my ambition caused a lot of poor decisions that weren't thought out or considerate of others. It has taken me a lot of soul searching to admit this truth, but admitting the truth meant that I was ready to make a change, and willing to ask for help.

Over the years, I've built up extreme confidence in myself, and as a result, my performance expectations consistently improved. While I am all about self sufficiency, my mindset caused me to run into the same issues over and over again. I would hit a wall and I struggled with asking for help regarding problems I did not understand or experience before. Instead of asking for help, I fell back on my ability to figure things out. It would take me longer but eventually I got it. I wasn't sure why it was so hard asking for help, and the truth is, at times it still is. It felt like a shot to my ego--asking for help felt more like being helpless or begging.

The tough love I received from my father and gave to myself made asking for help a worst case scenario. He is a prideful person, and many of us are. We have integrity, right? When someone offers to help you, do you feel like you owe them? Do you have a moment where it makes you feel helpless? That feeling causes us to act weird and say things like, "you don't have to", "I owe you", or "I hope I'm not bothering you", and maybe these are the right things to say. I was always taught to acknowledge those who chose to lend a hand in times of need. We can't do everything that needs to be done ourselves, and as much as I have tried to defy this statement, life continues to show me why it's true.

"Jose, let me tell you something. People actually like helping others, it gives us a sense of purpose." These were the words of my head coach in college and they have always been in the back of my mind when I'm searching for the courage to ask for help today.

THE ONE'S THAT HELP US

When an individual sacrifices their time to help you, it can be for a number of reasons or all the reasons at once. They know that helping you will serve themselves in the near or distant future. They have faced similar issues and could advise you on how to avoid those mistakes. They feel an overwhelming calling to serve and help others, and in return they feel great about themselves. Whatever a person's reason is, how you make use of the assistance is important because information alone will not help us.

Over time, those who we seek help from frequently become resources, the type of help that can be utilized across a wide range of problems. It has been in my best interest to know where those resources are, to identify them, and to use them often. As the problems in our lives become greater, there will likely be a need for newer resources, because the old ones may no longer serve us.

People are resources: what they say, do, and create will determine how effective they can be at assisting others. You need to be serious, show a willingness to help yourself, and above all else, respect their time and let them know that you can be a resource to them.

You are strong, you are powerful, and your self expectations has you operating on a higher frequency than your peers. You've realized faster than others that your best resource may be yourself. If you've solved a similar problem in the past, despite your doubt you can solve that problem again. Although, this time, you may need to pick up the phone and call for help; it's time to outsource. Calling for help can be difficult but we must remind ourselves what matters most, and that's execution. This is about not letting yourself down again. You want to learn what it takes to execute, because your expectations are so high that if you don't execute, the self-punishment can be overbearing. You have spent time identifying and gathering information about potential help--now use it. Your way might not be the best way this time. I had to learn that if my help is inside, then things will be alright if I go out. If help happens to be outside, then going inside might be the better move. Knowing where your help is takes trust. Get help from people you trust and if you don't trust anyone, start there.

If you can't trust others to help you, there might be a reason. Perhaps there has been some trauma in your life that suggests that trusting others can hurt you. My entire life I felt like I was a burden to other people, so when it was time to ask for help, I didn't. I did not want to interrupt people's lives or "bother" them. Pretending I knew best, I went for it and fell on my ass over and over again. I've come to appreciate this style of learning, but the punishment takes its toll.

Build a team: a few individuals that will keep you centered. If you are ever falling, they will pick you up, and if you are getting too high, they will remind you of humility. As capable as I am, I know I need help, as we all do. Your team can also become books, podcasts, articles, music, professional courses, etc., as they all were created by people for your consumption and usage.

This step is critical when shifting your mindset. Don't try to be "self-made". Know what works for you, and identify and utilize the resources available to you. Sometimes it feels like there aren't any resources, nearby help, or assistance. In those moments, remind yourself that the biggest resource you have available is you. Knowing what you don't know can be empowering, and it will inspire you to search and find out what you feel you need to know. Somehow along our journey, we met the right people, go places, and collect knowledge and possession that propel us further. With the right amount of patience, we will create all the resources we need.

....

Never underestimate what you know, and with the help of what others know, you can be unstoppable.

....

Chapter 9:

"Coach me, Coach"

"Sometimes we do not know what we don't know"- Anonymous

On August 9, 2014, I stepped on the University of Rhode Island's campus for a training camp. I was determined to show the coaches and my teammates how hard I had worked on my body and my game since the last time they saw me during my official visit. The excitement and anxiously filled my heart: it was a new beginning, it was real now, I couldn't stop thinking about this moment on the train ride up from New York.

"Look at me, this city boy all the way up here in the middle of nowhere about to play division 1 football, this was a dream come true," I thought to myself. The game of football had taken me many places, but I knew this experience was different. This place felt more like a permanent change. I knew that walking out in four years; I would not be the same Jose that was walking in.

In the football world, we judge other players the moment we take a look at them. This was common--we were all competitors and so checking each other out to determine if a guy was "real" was extremely necessary. The scale we use to base our judgment was *"swag"*. Swag was how a person walked, talked, what kind of haircut they had, how they dressed, what kind of sporting gear they had and was it the Nike, Adidas, Underarmour, New Balance, etc. Each player had to go through the gauntlet of the eye test, there was no pass or fail, just whether you were a baller or not. This was our culture, and if you ask any football player you know today they will tell you the same, I promise.

As I walked into my first team meeting, I was amazed to see how 100+ guys could fit in such a small place. We all took our seats and began chatting and laughing; it was an exciting time for all of us. For many of us, this was the first time leaving our families to become part of a new one, a brotherhood. The "cool" guys were the loudest and with that came small verbal groups beginning to form, which was normal because we didn't know each other well enough yet. The eye test would be at an all-time high in the team meeting, and finally, everyone was in close enough proximity to be observed and judged. I felt some eyes on me, and I only hoped that my cool Adidas tracksuit, my tall posture, and Nike backpack were earning me some points on the eye test so I played it cool and engaged in some conversations.

The room went silent as the head coach walked in. He was about 6'3, wide, and had a slight forward lean to his walk. Coaches were certainly under the same rules of the eye test as the players, and the moment he walked in we all knew that this guy had knowledge and years of coaching experience. The moment Coach Fleming opened his mouth to address the team, his midwestern accent came pouring out. I was from New York City and this was the first time I'd had someone address a large group with such a strong accent. We had met during my official visit but he didn't sound as raspy then. I wondered if maybe it was because there were parents around.

When a coach has that midwestern accent, you know he was raised on football, you know he has been around the game for quite some time. Coach asked us all to take our hats off, sit up in our seats, and give him our eyes, so we did. "I'm excited to have you all here together...I don't care what school you come from or what offers you've all had because everyone has to earn a spot on this team," he said while staring us down.

This was refreshing to hear because based on the eye test, I could tell a lot of those guys were already into their junior and senior years in the program. Traditionally, this meant they would get the first shots at starting positions on day one of camp. It was a new year, new coaching staff, new standard and we all were starting from day one, so egos had to be surrendered because Coach Fleming didn't care for them.

Now that the standard was set, we all knew the next four weeks would bring considerable uncertainty. We all headed out for our first practice the following day, and it was clear that egos were filling the air like a thick fog. Guys sported their high school cleats and shirts under their new practice jerseys. Conversations about high school achievements and college offers were amongst some of the most talked-about things before the whistle blew. I couldn't help but feel out of place because NYC wasn't known for its football, let alone division 1 football players, so to brag about my accomplishments and the championship I had won would certainly not be respected. As the practice went on, a few guys lived up to their eye test results and others fell short of them, but it was hard to tell where the talent was in shorts and tee shirts.

Coaches were teaching day 1 football stuff, the kind of day 1 teaching you learned when you joined your first team ever. Most of us had been playing football for 10+ years so being re-taught the most simple fundamentals again seemed like a waste of time. We were put through basic body positioning drills and general football mechanics. Coaches went over gaps, numbers, and formational strengths. Everyone would agree that this was the type of stuff you learned day one in peewee football.

It was not what I envisioned when I thought about my first practices at one of the higher levels of college football. It became very clear that the coaches didn't care about any of our opinions regarding his style of coaching on day one and he made it clear after practice. Based on the body language he had gotten from many of us, he reflected that he hoped to coach players who wanted to learn, who wanted to be good ballers, who wanted to play for the university.

He used three words to summarize the type of attitude he taught the game to, and that attitude was a "coach me coach" attitude. After that day, the phrase would be said by other coaches in the following practices. It was almost like they wanted to create a bunch of coachable robots. We all had an idea of what it meant: they tried to coach players who had an overwhelming desire to learn and be coached. I assumed every player had that approach, or we wouldn't be playing college football. The coaches wanted their players to be eager every day to come to practice to learn and improve. While this type of attitude is one that surely has worked for many players, on the toughest days it can be difficult to follow through. Bad days in the field were frustrating. We would be so frustrated that sometimes we took it out on one another. Our bodies took a beating every day, and someday we had no enthusiasm at all to practice physical. After two weeks, every guy was mentally tapped out. All the practices, meetings, and film study became a repetitive nuance. However, when those four weeks were up, you were sure to be tougher, smarter, and a complete football player. We all left camp with full heads of hair, bruises all over our bodies, and most of us were sick of hitting the same people every day. We were all ready to put our hands on an opposing team and see how we measured up.

In my mind I knew I wanted to be a really good player, but I wouldn't tell anyone because I was afraid of the accountability that came with others knowing my vision. Although they may not be the ones to tell me to my face, I would have to be ok with someone else knowing. To avoid the guilt of not taking action on my visions I felt compelled to work hard and give my goals energy and it benefited me greatly. I have always had high expectations for myself and sometimes wondered why. As many times as I tried, I was never considered the best at anything. But somehow, I always felt an extreme urgency to accomplish each goal. While I felt courageous for taking action, the quality of each accomplishment was average at best. I always expected the final product to be nothing short of a masterpiece, and I was sadly mistaken.I couldn't seem to allow myself to lower expectations or "take a reality check". I always seemed to be amongst the above average performers of the group, not the type of performers that were talked about in the school newspaper or post-game stat reports. I did my job, played my role well, and was always a productive member of the team. In my heart, I desired more. I didn't know why but I just did.

Do you know the feeling of just being good enough to get by but not being able to stand out amongst your peers? Some people will call it cockiness, overconfidence, or being full of yourself. Few will understand your standards and that is okay. All my life I have struggled with this, and I knew that to free myself from routine disappointment, I needed to adopt a new mindset. Feeling impatient all the time resulted in low-quality outputs, and I needed to make things simple.

I began searching for a way to achieve simplicity. I learned about people who were able to reverse engineer projects and how they did it. I was desperate to know what I needed to do to escape average outputs. I listen to credible personalities, read self-help books, and binged watched TEDx talks on youtube. No option was off the table. After all the digging, I learned that I had to let go of everything I thought to be true. In the words of Coach Rektis, I had to be "reborn again."

BEGINNERS MIND

Shoshin is a Zen Buddhist word I heard from a gentleman at my job one day who became like a mentor. He asked me to look the word up and come back to him the next day. Each day he would come to the gym, sit in the waiting area to read for about one hour, then proceed to exercise for the next three hours. Afterwards, he would shower, engage in some conversation with the trainers, then head out for the day. This was his routine and he did this every day. I was amazed at how a person could spend over five hours in the gym every day. After a few conversations, I learned that he had earned his financial freedom and enjoyed taking care of his mind and body this way.

The next day, I came back to tell him about the word. The previous night I read many articles and watched dozens of videos on its origin and meaning. *Shoshin* means "beginner's mind". Shoshin refers to the idea of letting go of your preconceptions and having an attitude of openness when studying a subject. As true beginners, our minds are free of habit and we are open to all information. As we develop, so will our knowledge and we will naturally begin closing our minds to other possibilities. New information is harder to penetrate our already developed beliefs, and at that point, our perceived expertise is holding us back.

I was amazed at this word. It put everything into perspective for me, and when I returned to tell him what I had learned, we spoke for about an hour. I began to reflect on my time in college when I transitioned from thinking I had it all figured out to surrendering what I thought I knew for new information. I accepted that I was stepping into a new level of my life. I recognized there were people in place to prepare me for that level.

Whatever previously worked, may no longer be effective. I surrendered my ego because my way kept getting me the same results, and in this case, the results were never as fulfilling as I had expected. I gave myself over to my coach, I let my guard down, and I tried to learn the game of football all over again from a new perspective. This was the first time I had adopted an open mindset and was willing to admit that what I knew didn't matter anymore. Remember when I told you that each level of achievement is directly correlated to effort, sacrifice, and execution.

Truly adopting a beginner's mindset took considerable effort. Your ego will not let you off the hook that fast, and situations will rise to the test if your old way of thinking has passed on. I needed to sacrifice time with other interests so that I could spend more time with my coaches. We began studying football longer. I spent a lot more time going over gameday assignments and being more deliberate about taking better care of my body to perform those responsibilities better. Previously, I ate whatever and whenever I felt like it, and I had poor sleeping habits. I began learning increasing strength and muscle meant I needed to be intentional about my nutrition. The effort and sacrifice would mean nothing at all if I didn't show improvement.

Execution matters, I will break down why in a later chapter. *Execution is always the goal.* You have high expectations for yourself because you respect what execution represents: discipline, intention, and vision. The feelings of accomplishment because you executed your visions are priceless.

I believe in the power of good coaching because I have benefitted from having a coachable attitude. In college, I had not learned the importance of asking for help and so I consistently underperformed. Fortunately for me, I was now a collegiate athlete, and the coaches' job security heavily depended on the performance of their players, so it took effort *not* to receive the help that was available to me. I surrendered my ego and gave myself over to my coach. He taught me new ways of approaching performance: it was in- depth, almost like professional athletes. Trusting him was one of the smartest choices I made in college because at the end of my junior season, the accolades and recognition began rolling in and it felt good.

When I became a trainer, my friend and mentor would observe my sessions often. He took a liking to my coaching style and how I worked with clients differently. He always commented on how my client improvements were very noticeable and how often they came in to see me. I always took pride in how frequently my clients booked their sessions each week. One day he overheard me coaching my client on the fitness floor. I often informed my client that in order to make any changes to his body, he needed to trust me and give himself over to my coaching. Today, this is something I tell each new prospective clients when we began working together. I have the best intentions for them and want them to achieve their fitness goals as much as they do. I'm ultimately invested in the success of those who decide to feature me in their fitness journey. I would try to make it a rewarding experience, and all I needed was for them to show up. After overhearing my conversation, my friend and I spoke that afternoon, and he introduced me to *Shoshin*. This word began to solidify my mindset whenever facing new challenges and overcoming obstacles that felt impossible in the beginning.

I knew it worked, and now I was the coach and my job heavily depended on the satisfaction of my clients. My clients knew that it would take a lot of effort to NOT receive the help that I made available to them, as my goal has always been to serve them. This felt all too familiar. I knew this feeling because I was in their shoes not many years ago. Many clients have trusted me and some haven't, and I'm sure they have their reasons. Whether they executed their goals or not is entirely their choice and I understood quickly that I was merely a guide, a source of direction.

The same is true for you: if you've been living with disappointment but somehow cannot escape repeating the same behaviors, it may be time for a mindset shift. Whether you decide to get a mentor, read a book, listen to a podcast, take a course, or hire a coach of your own, you will need to trust. Albert Einstein said, "the definition of insanity is doing something over and over again expecting different results." If your way is not getting you the results you need, STOP! This step in your journey is about adapting the mindset needed to overcome disappointment and experience the joy of execution. Spend some time deciding on a path, be clear about what you want, and become a beginner again.

Shoshin!

Chapter 10:

Stand Tall, Proud Chest

"You have to be able to accept failure and get better."- LeBron
James

"The rookie personal trainer of the year in the companies goes to Jose Duncan from Crunch Union Square!"

The room filled with applause, and for a moment I felt my heart stop. I looked at my girlfriend and her smile eased my anxiousness. Everyone in the theatre looked around for me. I sat at the very top row and it was a long way to the bottom of the theatre to accept my award. With every step down the stairs to the bottom, I held back tears, I held back my urge to smile from chin to chin. I played it cool, at least I thought I did. Up until that point I had never been recognized as the best to do anything, I never received recognition for my performance that way, and the feeling was odd. I felt confident and accepted the fact that I had earned this award and maybe I deserved it. The room was filled with top trainers in the company, and I felt like I was joining the group of individuals who were exceptional at their craft. I had become an exceptional trainer in 2019 and finally I was unafraid to admit it.

Just a year ago you could have found me at that very award show watching everyone receive awards for their great ability to sell personal training. I thought to myself that I was capable of doing the same, I wasn't sure what it took, but I knew I could be a really good trainer. My expectations have always been high, but the confidence was blind. It had no substance, no prior execution to drive it, but still I knew that I wanted my name called too and be known as one of the best.

On February 22, 2019, I walked into Crunch Fitness in Union Square Manhattan excited to begin my first day as a personal trainer. 22 days prior I had been cut from playing professional football with the San Diego Fleet, a team that was a part of the Alliance of American Football League. 22 days ago I was told that I wasn't good enough to be a contributing member of a football team, and 52 days before that I lost my stepmother to congestive heart failure. My mind had been uneasy for weeks. After my stepmom's passing, the pressures of making a professional football roster didn't make my situation any better. I walked into my first day of work determined to regain my confidence. Due to the recent events, I had lost it, I was frustrated and unfulfilled with how my life was going. I knew that I needed to rise again.

I felt that my slate had been wiped clean and I had a second chance at deciding who I wanted to be. The words of the general manager from the team who had cut me echoed in my mind, and as much as I thought I was ready to move on, I wasn't.

"We are going to let you go Jose," he said without looking me in the eyes. I couldn't be upset at him, it was his job to say those words to 30+ men who were hoping to further their football careers with the team. I stood silent in the GM's office, confused, angry, and feeling like I wanted to cry.The general manager reached across the desk and handed me my final payment in an envelope. In exchange, I gave in my playbook as he was making it clear that I no longer needed it.

The envelope felt heavy, and my heart was broken. I desperately wanted to ask why I was being let go, but I didn't. I just spent the last 30 days practicing day in and day out with the team, I showed up every day prepared to work, never missed a practice or a meeting. I ate with the guys, built strong relationships, laughed, and shared the love of football with them, and with just a few short words, it all came to an end. In that room with the general manager, I felt misunderstood. Maybe he didn't know about my relentless work ethic to get better, maybe he didn't know about how durable I had become, and how I would do everything that was needed to be available to play and contribute. He didn't know I was a leader, that given time I could help my teammates perform better and unite them.

On the plane ride home I wondered what life would be like without football. Football had always been home, and suddenly I felt as if I was being exiled. My confidence hadn't taken a hit just yet; my dissatisfaction kept me in denial for the days following being cut. I thought to myself that this might have been a sign from God, that maybe I was called to do something different. Have you ever felt like a failure and instead of facing it you tell yourself it's a sign from "God"? Maybe it is a sign, and we just choose to interpret it the way we want so we can feel less pain. Somehow, the interpretation is that it's not our fault, but the doing of a more powerful force in the universe.

. . . .

"The truth is a hard pill to swallow".

. . . .

When everyone asked me how things went or why I got cut, I used excuses like "I was last on the depth chart", or "it's politics". I needed to justify why I was home and not playing professional football. I hid the fact that my confidence was shattered like broken glass on a kitchen floor. There I was, tiptoeing around the broken pieces of my heart, trying not to step on a shard of glass because I didn't want to bleed again. The 21 days before walking in the door to begin my new life as a trainer, I wasn't sure who I was. I had no identity and it scared me. My fear of living without purpose had resurfaced. I spent days watching motivational videos, listening to podcasts, and searching Google for answers to my problems. I found nothing, the truth was that getting cut was indeed a sign from "God", a sign that needed to come in this form, or I would have never paid attention to it. The truth was that I wasn't good enough. Not emotionally or socially, but I wasn't good enough when I needed to be. The overwhelming fact was I did not perform well enough to earn a spot on that team. In those 30 days, I needed to be at my best and I wasn't. I needed to outperform other players, and I didn't do it exceptionally enough. It didn't matter that I felt misunderstood, the only thing that mattered was that I failed to execute.

I've always been just good enough, never exceptional, never consistent with my outputs. Do you know the saying "the truth will set you free"? I felt free when I admitted it to myself, but the truth had a way of creating so much pain that you don't feel free at all, the truth can feel disabling.

On my first day of work, I didn't know what it took to win the rookie of the year awards. I didn't know what it was like to be featured in fitness articles or sell over 120,000 dollars in personal training. The only thing I knew was that I needed to regain my confidence, and the only thing on my mind was executing. I needed to perform. I didn't care how I was going to do it. I needed to generate some good outputs so that my confidence came roaring back. I showed up early, stayed late, talked to almost every member in the gym, asked questions, and did whatever was required so that I could grow my training clientele. My business grew, the money didn't matter, and neither the recognition from others who praised how quickly I was able to build my business. The only thing I was in search of was proving to myself that I was good enough, that I could execute when it was time to perform.

For months, I was killing it. I sold thousands in personal training, and changed the lives of my clients every day. Somehow, after all the accomplishments I couldn't shake the feeling that I wasn't good enough yet.

Being cut was traumatic. My expectations have always been high, but I couldn't help feeling like I indeed let myself down. However, today I can assure you that there is one thing that is certain: lowering personal expectations is NOT an option! So many people were quick to lower them for me when I returned home. Honestly, they had every right to--it's what you do to make others feel better about not getting what they want, right? The overwhelming truth was that it was up to me to show them the hunger I had inside me that refused to quit. A few clients would always remind me of the impact I've had on their lives. They always express the quality of our sessions and how great they felt afterward. Still, it wasn't until a year later that I acknowledged myself as good enough while receiving an award. For the first time in my life, I accepted that I could truly set high expectations and meet them: *it just took patience and the right attitude.*

When I was a young kid, my coaches always told us, "Son, stand tall, proud chest," when we were at our most exhausted points. I never understood why, for this made it difficult to breathe. But, after a while we were able to slow our breathing down, open our eyes, then refocus on the task at hand.

Standing tall with our chest proud was a way of showing our opponent that we were strong, well conditioned, and most of all, CONFIDENT. As I got older, I realized that confidence is not about our opponents. Rather, confidence is about how we feel about ourselves and how we handle challenging and uncomfortable situations. Confidence is a journey of each person to take alone, and the last thing we want is for others to decide how confident we can become. Others are not our concern, first we need to prove it to ourselves. Only we can decide when it's time to raise our expectations and only we have the power to do what is necessary to meet them.

....

"People don't fail because they aim too high and miss, but because they aim too low and hit." - Les Brown

....

A SPECIAL TYPE OF CONFIDENCE

By definition, confidence is the ability to have "a feeling or consciousness of one's powers or reliance on one's circumstances." Feeling prepared generates confidence. I've learned this from being an athlete during my teenage years. Having a willingness to do whatever is necessary is a rare trait. To have a shot at a particular outcome meant you were confident in your willpower. There is a powerful kind of confidence that is deeply rooted in our high expectations. The belief in one's ability to figure things out may be the most important type of faith to possess. Perfectionism will prevent this type of confidence from manifesting itself. This type of confidence is quiet; it's not driven by external fulfillment. Instead, it's an internal trust that *no circumstance is greater than your determination to overcome it.*

This type of confidence is learned with experience, and it requires you to have come out on the other side of struggle and failure stronger and still standing. It requires wisdom and patience. It is the kind of confidence your grandmother has from living so long and experiencing so much. It's the kind of confidence an

137

Olympic athlete has before they compete. Somewhere along our journey we are met with unexpected circumstances that we haven't prepared for, and although our behavior may change, we still keep moving. We know that sometimes just getting through difficult times indicates that you are getting better. Only faith, and a commitment to take things day by day will build that special kind of confidence.

What does it feel like when you are executing at a high level? Do you feel empowered, certain, and determined? What is it like when everyone's acknowledging you for your efforts? Take a moment to remember those moments in your life, remember the setting, the people, the age, and what you were being recognized for. How have those moments shaped your confidence?

As an athlete, it's common to experience constant changes in confidence. You must deal with the personal struggles that come with preparation, and your team is affected as well due to the outcomes of competitive matches. I played 42 out of 44 games in college, and out of those 44 games, we won only seven of them. Some of the most embarrassing moments of my life came from being a part of a severely struggling football team, and in many of the games we weren't competitive at all. Our confidence as a team diminished, we felt incapable of winning competitive football games. Coming out on the losing end of hard-fought matches took its toll on both players and coaches.

We practiced next play mentality often, it was difficult, but we had to move on to the next opponent. Within 48hrs of getting our butts kicked we needed to find a way to get our confidence back and practice again. Today I don't know how we did it, but we did, and when we finally executed and earned a victory, we celebrated loud, hard, and together. It was there where I learned the power of persistence. Looking at my teammates in the eyes after losing and seeing them broken inside, I learned what love truly was. Being a part of so many losses and very few wins made me appreciate the wins so much more. It was in those moments I discovered that "special" kind of confidence. I developed a strong belief that even when I'm losing, I would eventually figure out how to win.

In our journey of overcoming disappointment without lower ing expectations, we must practice confidence. You will likely lose confidence after an unsuccessful attempt at earning something important. When this happens we must first work at overcoming that feeling of letdown to discover confidence again. Confidence becomes a practice; you learn how to generate it by completing tasks, following through on your plans, and helping others. When do you feel you're most confident? This is an important question to ask yourself because knowing when you feel you're most confident will become a personal resource for you to use when things aren't executing as you planned.

I encourage you to stand firm in discomfort as well, as conquering uncomfortable situations will help you develop the special confidence. The kind of confidence that is reassuring because you know that you're capable of figuring things out no matter the circumstances. I will also encourage that when you feel like everything is out of control and the pressures of life become too much, stand tall with a proud chest.

Confidence is not a step in our journey, it doesn't merit completion. *Confidence is a lifestyle and it's up to us to give it life every day.*

Part Two Summary

Mindset Shift

"What you're thinking is what you're becoming." – Muhammad Ali

By now, your practice of self awareness has taught you that your mind is a lot more powerful than you once believed. All human behavior can be broken down into four central emotional states. Happiness, Sadness, Fear, and Anger, and these four emotions cause three major effects that will normally follow. Happiness is followed by reward, sadness followed by punishment, and fear and anger are followed by stress. For each emotion there is an equal reaction that influences action and important decision making. Mindset shift is about learning proper utilization of those reactions in order to generate desired outcomes. As personal expectations rise, so will the desire for happiness and reward.

However, fear and anger will increase levels of stress when attempting an important task. Sadness is the feeling we feel when we fail to execute or others let us down, and self punishment almost always follows in some capacity.

Every emotion serves an important role, and it's up to us to decide the role they play based on the circumstances in place. Having a "coach me, coach" attitude means you are open to learning and forming new ideas. Welcoming new perspectives can cause fear and deep uncertainty about embracing new ideas. However, there is great value in the uncertainty because we grow too accustomed to our previous thinking as time goes on. The shift happens when we acknowledge that fear and press on in-spite of it. As we try to find what works, we may be surprised to realize that anger is key to execution. There are many friends I know that use anger from past trauma or unpleasant experiences to motivate them to make a change or complete a demanding task. Sadness and anger exist. We have no control of their existence, but how we use it is completely up to us. By now we've learned that all things require persistence. Repeating a behavior consistently increases your chances of execution and even mastery. Repetition of positive behaviors can lead to happiness and due reward, but repeating poor behaviors can result in sadness and self punishment. We all are in the driver's seat. No one is perfect, and at times the best mindset needed is one that is able to just move onto the next play. Whether the outcome was good or bad, the ability to regather your thoughts, reset your intention, and refocus are key character traits.

This journey is about you, but you don't have to go at it alone, identify where your help is and utilize resources available to you. The help will always be available, even in the toughest circumstances there is help available, so use it. Our minds are powerful forces that can either help or hurt us. There are so many mental obstacles that humans must overcome and no person is exempt. In knowing this, it's vital that you practice confidence, the goal is to develop that special kind of confidence that you can get through anything. We have changed the way we look at our life, we have acknowledged what we have become, we are making the decision to think differently. It's time that our thoughts serve a greater purpose in our decision making, it's going to take some consistency.

If you're still reading, you've made the choice to overcome disappointment and self punishment and your mind is ready for change. For that, you deserve a lot of respect. There is no longer room for simply being interested in the change you're after, you need to become committed.

COMMITMENT

Chapter 11:

Just Show Up

"I've got to keep showing up every day and putting in work". -
Julio Jones

Do you have that one friend or family member who always wants to know what happened because they weren't there, and they seem so disappointed because they missed something cool or important? In your mind, you're always thinking, "if they would just show up then they wouldn't miss things!" However, the sad truth is that so many people rely on others to relay important information that they weren't present for. At times this is justifiable but I'm not here to debate about what's justifiable. If you are going to live with those high expectations you've set for yourself, then not showing up is not something you want to justify often. Not everyone has high expectations for themselves, and that's completely fine, but you have chosen to be different, so you are held to a higher standard of behavior.

Long before I was an award winning personal trainer, I was just a scrawny little kid who fell in love with the game of football. I wasn't sure what love was, but I knew that I never wanted to leave practice. I was obsessed because it was fun. That kind of love may not work for all circumstances where love is required, but as an athlete it was the perfect romance story. When you're in love with something, you tend to sacrifice your time with other things so that you can be around it more. When I was in junior high, I would leave school early to head over to practice. I would completely skip my final class of the day so I could catch the early A train that went from Queens to Brooklyn.

At 2:00PM the bell would ring for the 8th period. It was the last school period and quite honestly, it was the worst because after lunch everyone was mentally tapped out. I would store extra chocolate milk and peanut butter and jelly sandwiches in my uniform pants pocket on the days I knew I was sneaking out early. Going to school in Queens and playing for a football team in Brooklyn meant I had an hour train ride every day, and when I didn't get allowance money from my parents, I needed to find a way to eat on the trip.

When I knew I was going to sneak out, I made sure to leave the back door to the lunchroom propped open during lunch period because I knew school security turned off the alarm system so that we could play outside.

During class periods, if the doors were opened it would trigger the alarms and the security guard would know right away that someone left through the side doors. I couldn't simply walk out the front door, as school security sat there all day and the moment I tried to leave I would get in big trouble. Kids cut classes all the time, so not being present during class time wasn't ok, but the teachers knew it happened. Right after 7th period, I would make my way over to staircase J and slip out the side door. I would gently let the door close but I wouldn't shut it because that would have triggered the alarms and put an end to my plan. When I finally got out, I would begin running down the street to catch the 2:06pm train to Brooklyn. You could have found me sprinting full speed down the road in my button up white shirt and dress pants--I was a mess. I felt so badass. I just wanted to get to practice early and many days I did.

When the report cards came out at the end of the quarter, I had 20+ absences, as much as I tried to hide it from my dad the teachers would always let me down. Most teachers took attendance in the first period, so I alway made sure I was present for it. However, some teachers were evil enough to take attendance last period as well. Not all teachers did because if that was the case, the absences would be up in the 40+ range easily. My social studies teacher was the culprit for this betrayal, and after being whipped by my dad for missing her class 20+ times she saw me a lot more. I never liked her before that and now I disliked her so much I wouldn't do her work, caused trouble in the class, and decided that my longest bathroom break was during her class. This went on for weeks, and my coach began to ask me why I wasn't early to practice anymore. I felt ashamed.

I thought he wasn't aware that I had been cutting classes to make it early, so I lied and said I wasn't catching the same train anymore. I hadn't yet known my dad already informed him of what I was doing and how it affected my education. As a punishment for lying, coach decided to suspend me for 3 games. I was devastated and embarrassed, and I wondered what my teammates would think about me when I wasn't at practice anymore. Coach decided to send me home that day.

Before I left the field, Coach Bill called me over and made me tell the team that I was cutting classes and wouldn't be around for some time because of it. Before I jumped the gate to walk to the train station I started to cry. The disappointment was too much to bear. I thought I was doing the right thing but I wasn't, and that was clear now. Just when I made it to the gate a voice called out, "Jose get back over here, I wasn't done with you!"

It was Coach Bill, and I made my way over to him in hopes that maybe his mind had changed and he forgave me, but instead he asked me to hand in my equipment so that another kid more deserving could use it while I was gone. He sat me down in the equipment shed afterwards and proceeded to give me some of the most impactful advice I have ever gotten.

He said, "Son, I'm disappointed in you, your dad is disappointed in you, now you let your teammates down, and you are crying because you let yourself down. I'm not suspending you from the team because we don't need you, you're being sent you home because you're a knucklehead. Your education is important and you don't know how much you may have disappointed that teacher, and you owe her and your father an apology. Next time you need to be somewhere, you make it a job to be there. People are depending on you to be there."

His words penetrated my 14-year-old mind. I didn't understand what he meant by just "being somewhere." I didn't know why it was important to show up to something that I didn't enjoy for the sake of just being there. I loved practice and never missed one, but 8th period of middle school didn't really make the cut for me. I knew it was wrong, but if it meant I was early to practice to help set up the equipment with the coach then so be it.

I loved playing football with my teammates, and now I was forced to be away from them for three full weeks and it killed me. The pain of not being a part of the team was greater than the pain of sitting through the last class of the day. I knew my team needed me and that was where all the disappointment rooted from, not being able to contribute because I decided to not show up to class. I stopped leaving the lunchroom door propped open, after lunch I went right up to class like everyone else, left when I was dismissed like everyone else, and did things the right way for a while. After the 3 weeks of doing the right thing I returned to football. I hated the new normal, and I would arrive at practice with little to no time to collect myself and needed to change and go right into it.

Long gone were the days I would hang out for 40 minutes before practice kicking it with teammates and coaches. My relationship with the social studies teacher improved: she saw right through my poor behavior and asked me to respect her and stop embarrassing my parents. She was a tall Jamaican woman who understood how important education was to immigrant West Indian parents. She became one of my favorite teachers I ever had. She helped me get out of suspensions and even let me lead class projects. When my behavior got a lot better, she would actually let me out early so I could head to practice. She informed the security guards at the front desk that she would be letting me out early, and some days and I was able to walk right out the front door. It turned out that sticking around to the end of the day I was able to meet a friend's dad who drove him home and offered to drop me off closer to Brooklyn so I didn't have to rush for the train anymore. He became an absolute blessing that school year.

I started showing up because if I didn't; I would lose the only important thing. I showed up because I never wanted to let my teammates down like that again. I showed up because each year my dad spent hundreds of dollars on football for me and I needed to show my appreciation. I showed up because I never wanted to be sent home from practice with tears in my eyes feeling like the world was crashing down on me because I made a mistake.

Today I reflect on that experience, and it was a small price to pay for such an important lesson, but when you're a kid it doesn't feel like that. When we're kids, having the most important things taken from us so that we could learn important lessons seems unnecessary and extreme. What we learn is more important than what we have.

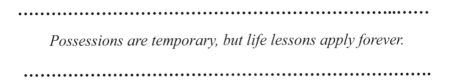

Possessions are temporary, but life lessons apply forever.

When we feel that something doesn't serve us directly, we are quick to dismiss it entirely. The discomfort we associate with it convinces us that it serves little to no purpose in our development. As intuitive and intelligent as we are in our decision making, sometimes we are wrong, and some things may serve us in ways we didn't think we needed serving. Your expectations are so high that you feel you can't waste time on things that don't push you forward immediately. Sometimes as we take 5 steps forward we need to take 10 steps back because we were walking so fast that we missed important lessons along the way. There is only one way to truly know if something serves us: we must show up and experience it for ourselves.

Sometimes we try so desperately to avoid disappointment because we know how much we will punish ourselves. The regret can sometimes be too much to accept. You must at least give yourself a chance, being present in when and where you need to be will decrease your likelihood of encountering self disappointment. In some cases, showing up can still result in enormous amounts of disappointment, but how would you have known? Sometimes being at the right place at the right time is all you need to get the ball rolling. Some call it luck, but by showing up, you create your own luck.

....

"80 percent of success in life is just showing up." - Woody Allen

....

Living with high expectations and fighting self disappointment at the same time is exhausting: you always feel like you aren't doing enough. The ambition and hunger for success becomes very demanding. At some point we must commit ourselves to something, we must believe in an action that will advance us further to our goals. Before we can make any important decision as to what we plan to do, our presence is needed, without a focused intention with attention we can fall off-course. As a fitness coach, when I meet new potential clients I make it very clear that if they decide to hire me as their coach, we become a team. I create a level of accountability that we now have to each other and the most important responsibility we have is to be present. I know that my clients are busy individuals with families and children--it would be insensitive to ask them to be motivated and fully prepared to take my coaching all the time. However, many are motivated and determined in spite of having so many responsibilities. That type of determination is what separates the clients who make great progress from those who struggle more often. Whether they struggle or not, I ask that they continue to just walk through the doors and to trust me as their coach. I ask them to trust my intentions and know that when we are working together on improving their health and fitness, they have my full undivided attention.

I learned the importance of giving someone your undivided attention from being a part of teams with amazing coaches who demanded the attention of their players. It is the universal sign of respect, to be fully present with someone. It lets them know you care about what is being said and done. The clients who find a way to show up consistently get the most out of my training, and in return, I gain more experience as a coach. When they walk through the doors I know that I have a responsibility to *turn it on,* and that mindset keeps me going even on my most tired days.

Showing up is not just about you. Sometimes people are secretly depending on you to show up because you bring them energy. Sometimes just seeing your face reminds them to raise their own standard because they don't want to disappoint you. Don't disappoint them, show up, be yourself and add value to their lives. Output matters, your performance matters, and showing up even when it's inconvenient for you increases your chances of executing. However, depending on what you are trying to accomplish, your presence alone will not be enough. Showing up is showing up with intention. You already did the difficult part and walked through the door but it's just as important that you focus. We all have things going on in our lives and we haven't surrendered our ego enough times to understand that others don't deserve the negative energy associated with our problems. You cannot expect to win if you are not willing to play the game. Winning requires contribution and to contribute you need to be there.

In our journey to overcoming self harm, it is important that we take time to heal. Healing happens within us ,but it doesn't need to be a solo journey. Connecting and building friendships and partnerships can be a daunting task for many people. In order to welcome those connections, oftentimes we need to make ourselves uncomfortable and vulnerable, and the best way to do it is to put yourself out there. Join groups, organizations, teams, companies, social groups, virtual chats, etc. Your presence in environments that benefit greatly from connecting with others will certainly increase your chances at finding like-minded individuals. When a group of people are connected to a purpose that's much bigger than any one person, it generates a lot of organic bonding. Everyone is seeking something, and so are you. There is an unspoken understanding that you need each other's help to find it.

There is no limit to how powerful genuine connections can be. If we don't make a commitment to showing up, then we can't give ourselves a chance. For many years I showed up to only things that required me to be there, where there were consequences if I decided not to show up. I feared the consequences, so I showed up, but I've always known I was doing the bare minimum. My effort to show up was average, therefore I continued to receive average results in my life. I've always felt I deserved great results. I wasn't sure why I felt that way but I did, and I don't feel bad about it either.

The universe was telling me to do better, to try harder, and to show up even when it wasn't convenient to do so. Just show up! It sounds so simple, and many will argue that it is--after all, it doesn't require much energy even if you're lazy.

Years ago in undergrad I was given some great advice from a mentor. He said to me, "The same reasons you'll have to show up, you'll have the same amount of reasons not to." The mind will not make it an easy choice, as so many things will stand in the way of you being where you know you should be.

An unwavering commitment to showing up is necessary. There is no shortcut for commitment. Commit your energy, your time, and your resources to do what you say you are going to do before the motivation wears off. Sometimes a commitment to a cause doesn't feel like an obligation, therefore you will need to commit to something or someone else. This way, your lack of effort to be present will have major consequences.

It's true your family needs you. Your friends do too, and your job certainly needs you to continue being a producing member of the organization. However, not until you show up for yourself will you ever be able to give those people the value you're capable of sharing. The choice is yours, so give yourself a chance. Make sure you're present and while you're there, make your presence felt.

Chapter 12:

Pain Has its Place

"Pain is weakness leaving the body."- Bill Solomon

I've had a total of six diagnosed concussions in my life. Those were so bad that I needed to be removed from a game or practice. Since I was 8 years old I've taken a sense of pride in always being available for my team. I was always ready on game day to play regardless of my physical condition. "Pain is weakness leaving the body, pain is weakness leaving the body, pain is weakness leaving the body" was a mantra I adopted from my pop warner football coach. When he first said it, I couldn't agree with him: to me, pain was just pain. Coach Bill was "rough around the edges", but a good man with good intentions. Unfortunately, he had a temper that would put the fear of God in us when he got angry. He was a Harvard educated businessman who left managing a company with 200 employees to start a youth football organization in one of the toughest places in Brooklyn, NY. I always wondered about Coach and how much physical pain he had endured in his life that he finally concluded that pain was just weakness and nothing more. He walked with an odd limp; he always told us about how he banged up his knees while playing, and I always imagined the number of injuries he must have experienced to permanently be left with a slight limp.

At 9 years old it's common for a young kid to complain and whine about feeling hurt or getting banged up. We ran into each other for 2 hours a day every day, so injuries were bound to happen. When a kid would get knocked down and hurt himself, Coach Bill would simply stand there and watch for a few seconds. He was a patient man that did not react often. After watching for a few seconds he would get angry if the kid stayed on the ground. He hated when we didn't get right back up to our feet and we all knew it. As patient as he was, he had zero tolerance for "wusses". It would set him ablaze and he would instantly demand that we got back to our feet and keep playing. When a kid finally built up enough courage and strength to get back up Coach Bill would say, "pain is weakness leaving the body."

Many parents hated when he did this. It was odd because afterward he would check on the player, talk to us, make sure we were ok, and asked if we needed anything before we headed home.

He was a great man and better coach. The only issue that many parents had with him was that he was willing to go to great lengths to teach lessons about toughness, and many felt it was unnecessary. His standards for us were so high that when one of us got hurt we wouldn't even inform him out of fear that he wouldn't care. As a result, many of us kept playing hurt or injured.

At 9 years old, you can play through the pain because you haven't yet discovered the purpose of pain, let alone what you do with it. We learn that from how others react to pain, we observe the choices that those around us make after experiencing pain. Growing up in rough poverty stricken neighborhoods, you see a lot of pain, and to deal with the pain, everyone is escaping their problems. It was common to watch older family members settling for instant relief with alcohol and drugs. Positive pain management role models were few and far in between and Coach Bill knew this all too well. He was determined to have no poor examples of pain management on his team even if it meant letting his players figure out their pain on their own before he stepped in.

I grew up in his system; it impacted how I handle pain. Today, I welcomed pain, I take it as a sign that once again I was shedding weakness. I have become obsessed with this shedding process. Long periods without experiencing pain worried me. I worried I would be getting 'soft' and my pain tolerance would reduce. This repeated behavior is one of the major reasons why I have such high expectations for myself today. I loved surrounding myself with others who also welcomed pain. It became a secret weapon that only a few athletes could discover and utilize. I knew that if I could continue to raise my pain tolerance then I would be able to perform longer and more effectively than my peers. Everything was about competition. We spent all of our time trying to outlast others and many knew that toughness was a key part of the puzzle.

PAIN IS WEAKNESS LEAVING THE BODY. This became the standard, the pain wasn't a sign to stop but instead an indicator that I was in the fight. I felt like a warrior on the football field. I used to say things like, "If I die, I want it to be on a football field." Before games, I would pretend that I was putting on armor like the vikings in all of the fictional warrior movies. When I walked out into the stadiums, I felt prepared for war, and in a way it was war. We weren't fighting over resources, but those 60 minutes were indeed bloody battles.

Studies show that out of every ten concussions related to sports, five of them go undetected or undiagnosed. I've had six diagnosed, which meant that I was messed up so badly that I needed to be told by a team doctor that I couldn't go back into the game. There are so many ways to hide a concussion and if it was so noticeable that the team doctors pulled you out of competition, then you got messed up pretty bad. As tough as I was, I could not ignore the pain of my head ringing and the temporary loss of consciousness. As an NCAA student-athlete, they take things like concussion really seriously. Team medical personnel would put us through a series of screenings and protocols if we even hinted that we might have felt concussed. Rightfully so, as the health of the players was a top priority and no one wanted to be liable for a player not receiving the proper medical attention.

Before I got to college I had only experienced three concussions, all stemming from poor tackling mechanics in high school. I lied about those during my physical when I got to college because I knew that if I told the truth I would be on the list of players that needed to be watched extra carefully. I was way too tough for that, and I desperately wanted to get playing time. I wasn't going to allow a team doctor to stop me. PAIN IS WEAKNESS LEAVING THE BODY.

At the start of my junior year, I had already collected the next three concussions during practices and one during a game; I was a warrior and those were just some battle wounds that I was able to bounce back from right away. When concussions did happen, I was removed from play, taken out of practice, and sent home with medication and a list of instructions on how NOT to use my brain so much. I didn't know what that meant. No video games was not an option; I wasn't the "lay down in the dark and do nothing for hours" kind of kid. Honestly, I am sure I never fully recovered from those concussions. Being listed as unavailable for my coaches and teammates wasn't a list that I appreciated being on. However, I did take full advantage of the letters that excused me from going to class, but not practicing or not being part of the game plan was unacceptable. By now, the medical staff knew that I wouldn't allow them to keep me out of practice. I would tell 'bald-faced' lies to be available on game day and still would today if I had to. There is a standard that comes with living with high expectations. As much as my team could use me, I knew that the person that needed me to play the most was myself.

I wasn't ok with watching from the sidelines because I was 'hurting'. Some guys did, but that wasn't me. Looking back at it today, I lacked self-awareness and should have sat some plays out to let someone else who was at full strength play. My standard was that even at my worst, I was valuable. I believed that even if no one else did. Some of the decisions were very selfish because I would be out there limping and barely moving fast enough to be productive. I wasn't perfect. My ego owned me and I knew it, but leaving the game felt like quitting and I am not a quitter. I built up such a reputation for "playing through the pain" that when I should've been replaced or given a break, my coach never recognized it. I feared that I would disappoint him if I came out of the game, and this fear of disappointment was one of my greatest weaknesses.

CONCUSSION NUMBER SEVEN

It was halftime during a hard-fought game with Stony Brook University. We had home-field advantage and the game was tight at the half. Emotions in the locker room were high because that team had always felt like our rivals during my time in college. They were really good trash talkers and played our brand of football--tough defense and exceptional special team units. They hit hard, their running backs were big and strong, and as for my defense, we LOVED to play physical. The physical matchups always took its toll on the players and collectively we all admitted each year that the Stony Brook Seawolves were the most physical team in our conference. They were so physical that the previous year I was diagnosed with concussion number six after the game, and it was one of the worst I ever experienced.

We entered the locker room at halftime with high energy. Guys were banged up but no one was taking themselves out of this one. Everyone wanted to be a part of tough battles that felt winnable. When I entered the locker room, something was strange. Before the whistle blew for halftime I went head to head with the running back and I swore he got the worst of it, but I was greatly mistaken. I walked directly to the bathroom and looked in the mirror. For the first time in my life I forgot where I was, and I felt confused and emotional. Concussions have this odd way of making me feel emotional; I always felt unsure how to feel and it bothered me each time I would experience one. In a locker room filled with players talking and coaches yelling, somehow I suddenly forgot why I was there. That feeling was undeniably one of the most frightening things I experienced in my 15 year of playing sports. My head was pounding, and I knew I needed to hide this because the moment the head trainer looked at me, he would have known right away my day was over.

I took a glance at the clock--we had seven minutes before we needed to head back on the field for the second half. I had to figure out what the hell was happening to me. I hid in the team showers trying to improvise ways to get back to reality. I turned on the shower-head and put my head under the cold water for a few minutes. I wasn't even sure if it was working but I was out of options. It became very clear that this was concussion number seven. Three concussions already, and I was only halfway through the junior year. If the medical team found out, I would be put on concussion watch until the end of my senior year. I couldn't risk that. I wanted to be on the field, I NEEDED to be on the field.

In the showers, I began repeating my coaches' mantra, "pain is weakness leaving the body," but this time the weakness never left. Instead, it got worse. The mantra always worked, but somehow in one of my most painful moments pain was not weakness, it was just pain. I felt anger as I began thinking about

Coach Bill. Was he wrong all these years? This moment was a clear indicator that when the pain wasn't ready to leave the body, it wouldn't, and it didn't matter how much I thought I was in control of pain because I wasn't. I wasn't sure what the pain was trying to teach me, but I had no time to reason with it.

"SECOND HALF LETS GO!", yelled the strength coach. It was time, it had become quite clear the shower water running on my head wasn't solving my problem, I turned off the shower-head and put my helmet on. It felt tighter, my headache roared, but at least with the helmet on I could hide my eyes because if you were to look in them they told a story of a player who CLEARLY wasn't ready to play another 30 minutes of football. I ran back on the field with concussion number seven, and I was frightened. I'd read stories about players dying on the football field, passing out, and even been paralyzed and I didn't want either fates. When the second half began, I knew right away I was making one of the biggest mistakes of my life by not informing anyone and deciding to play through it. My body felt limp. I was barely moving at half speed, and it was obvious.

When the officials asked me if I was ok, I found enough energy to nod my head yes. I wasn't sure why, but leaving the field meant I was a quitter. At least to me it felt that way. Perhaps I was being dramatic. I thought about that often and in response I tried my hardest to focus long enough to look like I was actually being a productive member of the team. The average play in football lasted about 5-8 seconds and with enough knowledge of the game, you can learn how to position yourself to seem active until the whistle blew. Up until that point I played so much football in my life that I would think of shortcuts often and inevitably it ruined my production. Coach Cogniglio was so used to leaving me out there that he never noticed I had not been ready to play the second half. No one was coming to save me, but at any moment I could have saved myself. But I didn't. Instead, I went on to play one of my worst football games ever.

The pain of such poor execution was greater than any of the seven concussions I had now endured. For days after the game, my choice to play the second half ate at me. At times I felt courageous and proud that I fought through it, and other times I felt selfish and stupid. In film sessions, my coach didn't hold back his disappointment either and I knew he was upset because he never had that amount of negative comments about my play.

Later that afternoon I informed him that I had a concussion at halftime and didn't tell anyone. I expected that he would understand and that it would justify such a poor performance. Instead, it was the complete opposite: he felt that not speaking up about the concussion hurt the team, that it was selfish and the act of an idiot. He explained that it wasn't what the leaders did; his disappointment shocked me. The pain had its moment during the game and I tried to cover it up and minimize it with a mantra, a shower, and tilting my helmet forward so no one saw my eyes. It wasn't courage that made me do it, it was fear. I feared my own expectations. I thought my team needed me and I didn't want to let them down. I needed them to count on me to be available and productive even if it meant I was not at my best.

Do you ever have those moments where you feel like you are needed by others? Doesn't it feel great? It's like the whole world is counting on you to fight and you'd rather fall on your shield than to drop your sword.

··

The truth is, the world isn't counting on you.

··

We make those things up in our heads to feel like we are serving a bigger purpose. The only person counting on us in those moments is ourself. We deny ourselves relief because somewhere along our journey we decided that we are the bearers of pain and that no pain is more powerful than our will. Some pain is ruthless, some pain is overwhelming, and some pain will make it extremely clear that it's in charge. Our expectations are so high that we welcome pain just so we can quickly "beat it". We aim to dispose of pain rather than concur it all together. Pain is no fool, and you might win the majority of the battles with your determination and will power, but PAIN is not a quitter either. The more you beat it, the harder it fights to retake its place in our lives.

It returns over and over again until it serves its purpose, but often we allow quick fixes to stop it from fulfilling its purpose. I HATE PAIN! As much as I welcome it when it comes, I still try to cover up all the entry points.

Pain has its place, and I had to accept this very harsh fact. Sitting in the same room with pain is uncomfortable. It's a staring contest to see who blinks first. Pain has its place, so make room for it in your home as it will come and go when needed. Don't try to change the locks or lock the windows, this makes pain angry and it will find a way in regardless.

Coach Bill said pain is weakness, and many times it can be. It will leave when we choose to let it run its course and we concur it. Pain and fear will always work together in our lives but we can choose their role. Pain has its place, but so does relief. In many cases, relief can follow painful feelings and those painful feelings never feel the same again. You are stronger because of the pain. We all are. There is no strength without overcoming resistance; to build new we must break down old.

Although pain certainly does serve a purpose, never welcome the same pain into your life consistently. If those same feelings continue to return then it may be time to reevaluate your choices and why they are leading you to the same mistakes.

This step of our commitment is about acceptance of pain. We must respect pain's role and welcome it so that we can learn and grow. As our expectations continue to grow we sometimes view pain as an indication that a setback is coming, and if we don't acknowledge it then it will. "I am in pain but..." is a simple way to acknowledge that it's there. It doesn't need to derail you. You've dealt with so much self- punishment, but it's time to commit to doing better. STOP ignoring your pain. It's there, work on it, use your resources. Use pain: it can become a valuable tool. On the other side of pain, there is something that you need to know, something that you must step into.

Acceptance of pain is a commitment because you will not always be able to accept it in the right way. It's going to take some practice and a series of recommitment efforts.

PAIN IS WEAKNESS LEAVING YOUR BODY, but only if you're willing to accept its presence.

....

"You're already in pain, get something out of it." - Eric Thomas

....

Chapter 13:

"If It Was Easy, Everyone Would Do It'

"It doesn't get easier, we get better." - Anonymous

I was an employed professional athlete for a total of 31 days. Day 32 was painful. Self disappointment and reflection cycled in my mind. It was an emotional rollercoaster. In the last 31 days, I had been reintroduced to discomfort, pain, and stress. This was all due to the high pressure environment that came with competing against 90+ others who all had the hopes of being on the right side of the 53 men that were kept on the team when the 31 days were up. I knew what pain was. I'd overcome discomfort dozens of times and learned some great stress management mechanics. Unfortunately, the things I knew was for the previous level of my life. I was transitioning into a professional now, and I knew it would require a new set of skills and habits so that I could give myself the best chance for making the team.

"PRO"

Sitting in the lobby at the team hotel in San Antonio, Texas was where I felt the most anxious in my entire life. I was 31 days away from officially becoming a professional athlete and all I could do in that moment was reflect. All the years of overcoming self disappointment led me there. I had a strong belief that I would figure it out. I knew that I needed to surrender my ego, I was the new guy again. I didn't know anything about this level of my life and hadn't earned anyone's respect yet.

Later that night, we had our first team meeting. I found out just how difficult the next few weeks were going to be. A combination of practice, film study, meeting, meals, study time, and recovery was the daily makeup of camp. Each morning my roommate Naim and I woke up more sore than the previous day. We made our way down to the breakfast hall to eat with the rest of the team and coaches, all of whom were either extremely fired up and ready to go or completely silent as they hadn't actually awakened yet. During the first week of camp everyone showed up to breakfast, sat together, and boarded the buses to practice together. It didn't take long before players began sleeping in, saving breakfast in their rooms, or skip breakfast altogether. Many former NFL guys choose to eat on the bus heading to practice, and maybe they knew something I didn't. Rest time became a privilege, and if you were really banged up from practice that morning, recovering your body for the following day of practice became a full time job.

The only day you feel fresh and completely energized is the first day of camp. After the first practice, everything changes and the body is transforming into what we called "football shape". Football shape isn't like any other fitness condition. It is a specific kind of shape that can only be achieved when wearing football equipment participating in actual game-like tempos and scenarios. One thing I carried over from college was the understanding that it was the job of the players to be ready to practice and play. We could not expect coaches to motivate us or ensure we made it to practice on time. As professionals, we all knew we had the sole responsibility to take care of our bodies. We're taught how to take ownership of our preparation, and each player was expected to make significant time investments. We were expected to sacrifice leisure time for performance preparation.

All athletes understand these truths: analyze any high-level athlete's behaviors in any field, and their actions make it clear. High level athletes in the game of football spend so much time, money, and resources to ensure that they recover the best they can. To them, performance matters and they all have an understanding that poor recovery kills performance. This was my first professional experience.

I knew very little about all the recovery resources available to me. I didn't go to a top power 5 conference school and wasn't exposed to the same knowledge and atmosphere. A lot of my teammates were former NFL guys who had either been on NFL rosters or just got released from one and seeking opportunities to get back. Only a handful of us had never made a roster and was hungry for our first shot at the NFL. Practices were competitive. If you weren't a first team guy, your reps would be very minimum so actually making them count wasn't some cliche term--it was crucial. Even the first team guys understood that their spots weren't secure either. One too many mistakes and coaches were prepared to replace them with the next guy.

Fighting for a job while the next man is waiting for you to make a mistake so that he got a chance at taking your job was merely the reality of football camp. Performing with very little room for error was expectations, execution mattered A LOT! Meetings were long and some days it was so hard to register all the information that was being shared. We relied heavily on each other to collect different parts of film breakdown. Later, that night we would ask each other questions about the upcoming practice plan to feel fully prepared. No one wanted to be the guy who missed a meeting or forgot a play installation. These types of mistakes were difficult to come back from, and if you were 2nd or 3rd on the debt chart, you avoided those mistakes like the plague. Coaches didn't expect everyone to be perfect, those expectations were unreasonable. However, if you wanted to give yourself the best chance of being around after the 31 days were up, your expectations had to be excellence.

Many long-time athletes will tell you that athletic ability sometimes made up for critical mental errors during a performance. However, it wasn't a gift that coaches wanted to use often. Have you ever needed to have very high personal expectations because you feared that one mistake would cost you everything? If you have, then you know that fear is exhausting. It repeats itself over and over again until we break. If you want to overcome this fear, proper preparation was the only remedy.

Preparation became more important than the action we were all preparing for and everyone from the coaches, players, and support staff knew it. At least if you did all you could to prepare your mind and body for performance then you could trust that you would make fewer mistakes. Many nights during camp I studied my playbook for hours and I watched films on well-known players in the NFL that played my position. I studied their postures, their movements, their effort, and their execution. I went through my own films play by play, critiquing my own posture, movement, and execution. It should be no surprise that I was never satisfied with the films. I have never been satisfied with my performance since I stepped foot into the University of Rhode Island 6 years prior. I never felt I was gifted with any particular talent of playing football, but I had a commitment to do whatever was necessary to compete with those who I felt did possess talent. Film study, proper diet, studying playbooks, and becoming more intentional about sleep were amongst the top priorities for players during camp.

As soon as practice was over, preparation for the next practice began immediately. Every second that passed after practice was considered preparation for the next opportunity. Everyone knew it, and those who didn't quite understand that didn't make it past the first week in camp and were sent home. If you needed ice to reduce swelling in your ankles or knees you were expected to be in the treatment suite after lunch. If you made a lot of critical mental errors during practice, coaches expected you to open your playbook and study. After positional meetings were over, you had better ask your positional coach to spend extra time with you going over your responsibilities. Players knew that making the same mistake twice was a guaranteed way to get dropped in the depth chart. Camp was so emotionally draining that at any time during the day you could find players calling home to speak with our families for moral support. Camp was 31 days of physical and emotional battles, but it was what made playing the game so sweet. The game came easy to most players: it was just a time to perform. Preparation and overthinking had no place there, it was an all-out fight.

No part of the process was easy, but it couldn't be. It needed to be difficult, it had to make or break us. "Football isn't for everybody," was a saying that my high school football coaches always said, and it has always been a saying that I embraced. The game of football is *not* for everyone, and being a part of a small population of players who embraced everything that came with being a football player was special. While the game isn't for everyone, the lessons and learned habits can help anyone. I was cut from the team because at that time I didn't quite understand one of the most important rules of competing at a high level and that was that EXECUTION MATTERS. Although my expectations were alway high, the expectations from coaches and the general manager were significantly higher. Even though I had limited opportunities, it was expected that I executed with maximum precision and focus. The results of my efforts needed to have an impact.

Many coaches had no expectations at all for young players like me. They invited us to camp because they felt we had potential, and it was up to us to surprise them. On day 30, I felt very optimistic about how I performed. On day 31, it turned out that my performance wasn't good enough to keep my job. This was the harsh reality I faced with 50+ other players. Sometimes it wasn't the right decision to let certain players go, and afterward, the coaches knew it. It's never easy to look at a group of 100 quality football players and let 47 of them go. That kind of job never gets easier.

"I CAN DO HARD THINGS."

The pain of being sent home cut deeply, but I walked out with my pride because I knew I was a good ball player--this time I just wasn't good enough. I would love to tell you a story about how I persevered and eventually had a breakthrough and made another professional roster but this isn't that story. I walked into one of the toughest job interviews and was willing to do whatever it took. I embraced every adversity, every struggle and did all the hard things without complaining. I expected that much of myself. I have always been committed to doing the difficult task even if I let myself down when I didn't follow through. Discomfort was my friend. I welcomed it because I knew that on the other side was something special. Having an unrelenting commitment to overcoming periods of discomfort to serve a greater purpose felt like a superpower. I knew that I could use this character trait as a competitive advantage in other areas of my life. IF IT WAS EASY, EVERYONE WOULD DO IT.

The biggest lesson I've learned from my experience was the importance of execution. In addition, the greatest gift I received was a newfound appreciation for doing hard things consistently. I knew that without football I had to reinvent myself. I needed to form a new set of practices and commitments. It has not been easy, but I despise being just good enough. If hard gets me greatness, then hard is the route for me. Striving for excellence is available to everyone, although the context of excellence depends on the person's expectations. Although available to everyone, not everyone will accept or qualify for the difficult journey. This step is about having a commitment to doing the difficult task in order to achieve your goals. We've done easy, and easy hasn't worked. We even dabbled with shortcuts, but those haven't created any sustainability.

You want it now, I get it. I've never had any patience and today I remind myself daily to have patience. It can be so tempting to choose the quick fix, 3 step manual, or an accelerated course. How we learn the information isn't the emphasis. How we apply the knowledge and the mental toughness required to last is most important. If you've come this far with high expectations for your life, it is not the time to lower them. Instead, it is time to create a practical plan to live up to them.

REMAIN HUMBLE

Commit to humility, and accept the fact that at any moment you can face adversity, your confidence will take a temporary hit.

Remember that you took the hard road, the one that leads to excellence. Be careful comparing yourself to others; this behavior will only frustrate you more. This battle is between you and only you. When I was released, I knew deep down I was a better football player than some of the guys who kept their jobs, and it ate at me for weeks. I had to live with that frustration and after a while, it no longer served the person I wanted to become.

THE RIGHT ENVIRONMENT

Disassociate with people who don't want excellence for you. If you consistently associate in low-frequency environments, doing hard things will eventually feel extra. I loved being around professional athletes because there was a consensus that we all had to embrace difficult situations to earn a spot. The environment itself brought out the best in me, exposed me to part of myself I had not yet discovered. YOU TOO CAN DO HARD THINGS.

"THE WALL"

This doesn't mean you run into a wall hundreds of times without any plan, it means that you're willing to find a strategic way to break through the wall. The walls in our lives are the challenges we are meant to overcome. They serve a greater purpose in our development. Don't be surprised if some of your peers see how big the wall is and turn back around--some will even try to sneak around. Many will also attempt to climb over with the right intentions, but they will not remain on the other side for long. Although they may see what's on the other side, they will fail to understand what they are seeing. There are lessons in the process of breaking that wall that we need to learn first. Information alone never changed anyone, but application produces understanding, and understanding requires patience. I know this because I've spent many years just trying to see the other side of hard work. I worked hard but my lack of patience always kept me from experiencing the breakthrough I so desperately needed. I was taught these lessons by coaches and mentors, but unfortunately my ego stopped me from applying those lessons. Instead, I learned the hard way every time, without fail. While there is power in hard-learned lessons, the experience can sometimes be very unpleasant.

•••

"You chose the hard road the moment you decided to go after your dreams." - Justin Sua

•••

DON'T FORGET, ITS A CHOICE.

Living with high expectations is a choice that can motivate us to take on difficult tasks and insert ourselves in complicated projects. Striving for excellence is also a choice. The game isn't fair, but we are playing it and that's the most important part.

A commitment to doing the hard things required can be extremely uncomfortable in the beginning. Not living up to your full potential will not make things better. It will leave you feeling so unhappy that the only way out of it is to embrace uncomfortable change. I learned from others the importance of doing the hard things. I spent time around them, asked questions and mimicked behaviors. To many of them, doing the difficult task wasn't always glorified but they did it anyway. The purpose behind their actions was bigger than their temporary feelings of pain. I was inspired by it and now I seek those types of people in my life regularly.

I encourage you to find those types of individuals in your life, listen to them, ask questions, and mimic their behaviors. If you possess the strength to motivate yourself to do the hard things, step into that strength. The world needs it. Who said you aren't the person that could lead others? Do you think you can inspire others to embrace discomfort because you've experienced your own journey with it?

....

If you think you can, you can.

....

Let people catch you in the act of doing hard things, standing tall in the face of adversity, and continuing to step out of your comfort zone. It's not showing off. People need to see it because we all are looking for inspiration. There is no one that thinks the way you think, there is no one who is like you because your life is unique. YOU CANNOT HELP EVERYONE. We control our intentions and actions but we don't control the impact. We only hope what our impact should be, and many times we are spot on. However, the truth is that all decisions are subjected to vast interpretations by others who know nothing about you, so do your thing and do it well.

In the words of Tom Hanks, "It's supposed to be hard. If it were easy, everyone would do it."

Chapter 14:

Make it Happen

"Some people want it to happen, some wish it would happen, others make it happen".- Micheal Jordan (6x NBA Champion)

By now, you probably have noticed how often I refer to execution. Even writing this chapter about how I discovered the power of execution feels redundant. Here is the truth--as painful as it is right now to admit it, I feel like it's time to outright come clean. All the self disappointment and self punishment that I have dealt with growing up could have been less emotionally damaging if I learned how to execute consistently. As I near the end of my first book, I still have moments when I struggle to open the laptop and write. So close to the end, all the work put in, all the chapters written, and still here I am struggling. It's taken me a few days to just admit to myself that I need to write a chapter about execution.

I felt like a hypocrite. How can I encourage action on something that I have struggled encouraging myself to do consistently?

THE TRUTH

The truth is I am not a guru, I am not an expert, and I didn't have the hardest upbringing out of my peers. I'm just a kid, 25 years of age, and filled with observed experiences and a heart full of ambition. Writing this chapter fills my mind with anxiety. This book is for you, the reader, to read my story and to reflect on your own. My goal is to encourage you to reflect on your own self punishment, pain, and disappointment. I want to encourage you to recognize that even after all the self beatdown and damage to your conscious, excellence is still available. People will tell you to lower your expectations, or to have no expectations at all. They are right to advise you as such, lowering expectations or having none at all can free your mind and increase your performance. I've tried this method, and it worked for a while. I got some things done and even surprised myself how good I was. However, a small little thought would crawl back into my head and disrupt that mindset. You know the thought I'm referring too. That thought is CONFIDENCE.

Confidence is the strong belief that we are capable, well equipped, and willing to do the hard things because we believe in ourselves. Once we see ourselves doing it, we cannot unsee it. The moment we feel greatness inside us, it's hard to just dismiss it. You stepped into the person you've been having visions about, that WHAT IF person actually showed its presence. YOU DID IT! YOU DID IT! YOU DID IT! Your family knows you did, your friends saw it, your coworkers experienced it, and most of all you felt it. Take a moment to imagine a time where you felt so accomplished because you overcame a lot of adversity to ultimately succeed in the end.

What did that moment feel like ? Who was there? What was the weather that day? What were you wearing? Where did you go? Please excuse me as I take a moment to participate in this practice myself and imagine my moment with you.

"ITS OFFICIAL"

Sitting in the Aqua Blue Hotel Main Conference room in Narragansett, Rhode Island on February 2, 2014, I was waiting to receive one of the biggest gifts of my life. Across from me at the table was Coach Fleming, the 6'2 New York native who recently left the University of Central Florida to take the head coaching job of a struggling URI program. I looked up to him for that, and I admired his body of work and how far he had come in his coaching journey. He made me feel like I was in a place that accepted and welcomed me, and it only took about 3 days to do so. Up until that point I had no full scholarship offers and I was desperate. This official visit was my last chance. It was four days before national signing day for college prospects and I wanted to be seated at the table signing my scholarship like the teammates who came before me had once done. It was a tradition to gather in the school library on signing day and sign our national letters of intent to go to the college of our choice. I wanted so desperately to be a part of that tradition. I always daydreamed about the moment so vividly, the parents, the media, and my friends all gathered to send us off.

Coach Fleming and I exchanged some small talk at the table about my experience visiting the school. I stuck my hands under the table so I could hide how badly my palms were sweating. I was nervous, and I needed him to say those words. My heart began racing when he began recapping his opinion of me and ultimately closing in on his decision whether he was saving my parents the burden of getting me to college.

For a few seconds the conversation fell silent, I could feel my body wanting to slip off the chair. The heat in the hotel was so high I could hardly breathe correctly. Coach Fleming leaned back into his chair, looked me in the eyes and said, "I would like to offer you a full scholarship to come play for me at The University of Rhode Island."

I wasn't sure how to respond, I felt I needed to play it cool as if I had been expecting this moment. The truth was that I was overwhelmed. I had never been handed a gift of that magnitude before. Coach Fleming sensed my uncertainty and hesitation to respond so he decided to follow up by asking me to verbally commit right there, on the spot. He stood up out of his chair and stuck out his hand to indicate we were coming to an agreement. I looked down at his hand and stuck my sweating hand out to meet his and said, "I'm committed."

February 2, 2014 was the day where all of the pain felt was worth it. The sacrifices made sense and the disappointing moments became important teachers. It was cold that day, snow was on the ground, and I wore my Timberland boots so that I looked taller than I was. I had on my grey Under Armour tracksuit that I wore almost everywhere with my all-black Adidas down coat. I remember this day vividly because it was the proudest day of my entire life.

It was the first time in my life where I had felt I actually made something happen. MAKE SOMETHING HAPPEN was a popular term growing up as an athlete because it was like a call to action--it served as words of encouragement that lead to execution. Up until then, I was always MAKING something happen but I just couldn't quite ever get to the finish line. I always had an energetic belief that I was capable of getting the job done, but somehow it always felt incomplete and unworthy of any approval. Accepting a full scholarship to a Division 1 college was the icing on the cake. It was no question that this was the embodiment of execution. The shocking reality was that it wasn't, instead it only served as the motivation I needed to truly EXECUTE.

What Coach Fleming didn't know was that just four months prior to my official visit, I wasn't eligible to play college football. At the time of the visit, I still had issues with eligibility that had not been corrected. My verbal commitment meant nothing because my GPA was too low and my SAT score wasn't high enough to pass clearinghouse. NCAA Clearinghouse was a matching system that compared your GPA to your SAT or ACT score to decide whether or not you were eligible to play college sports. If I didn't gain eligibility by the end of the semester, I wasn't going to play division one college football. My SAT score was too low but I knew that taking it again would not benefit me at all. Instead, I took a shot at giving all I had to my last semester to raise my overall GPA so that it balanced my overall clearinghouse score. That semester I MADE THINGS HAPPEN. I was on a mission, and many of my teammates were in similar predicaments. We all motivated each other to MAKE THINGS HAPPEN. Just getting by no longer served us anymore. Effort alone could not take the heavy burden off our parents to get us to and through college, we needed to become intentional.

My last semester of school, I never missed a day or a class. I had a full time job at Lowe's one hour away from my high school. At every level I was MAKING THINGS HAPPEN. No one was coming to save me, my parents didn't have the money, and I knew that my future was in my hands. Living with high expectations makes me embrace moments where I'm in control of my outcome. I realized that my effort, sacrifice, and execution could directly result in me getting the thing I wanted. There have been a few moments in life where I had that level of certainty about my future. Getting myself to college was a challenge that I accepted because I had never been tested in that way. I had never needed to be that strong. I took full accountability of my life that year, and now six years later I am living the results.

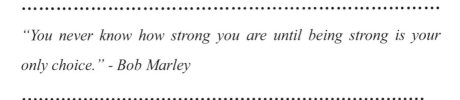

"You never know how strong you are until being strong is your only choice." - Bob Marley

"THE CLOSER"

When your back is against the wall, there is little room for retreat. It's reasonable to believe that your next move could be the wrong one but in your heart you know that you cannot stay there. The odds are 0/100 if you do not make a decision: your left and right sides are both closed off and the only way is forward. You either start moving forward or you stay where you are and suffer the consequences of complacency and dissatisfaction.

In my life I have always walked away from the wall, but I wouldn't get very far. I'd make substantial progress forward, but somehow never make it to the other side. Do you know what I mean by the other side? The other side is when you go through all the obstacles, make all the sacrifices to reach your goals. When you got there, you'd relish the moment, set new goals, and repeat. All my life I feared reaching the other side. I worried that if I did I would either not enjoy the moment enough or enjoy it too much. Therefore, I stayed in the "working phase".

Somewhere along my journey I stopped executing, and it's painful to admit. I'm a hard worker for sure, go getter certainly fits the description, leader has been labeled on me numerous times, but I knew the one title I desperately wanted the most. I wanted to be the "closer", the person who MADE THINGS HAPPEN. Do you ever feel like you know you're capable of making things happen but somehow it doesn't quite work out the way you imagined? Everyone praises you for your effort and energy but you know that your effort wasn't enough. I know this feeling eats you up inside, that you try to justify it, but the greatness in you won't allow it. I have learned that the ONLY way I can execute consistently is if I continue to move the wall up. My back needs to be consistently against the wall. Every few steps forward I needed to look back and see that the wall was continuously moving with me. That wall needs to be there until we reach the other side, only then can we defeat the greatest enemy: ourselves.

The wall I am referring to is the driving force for why we do things, it's the motivation that leads us to action. Your wall is whatever you decide it should be; everyone's purpose will not be the same. Everyone has their own WHY, and whether big or small, it's theirs and learning how to tap into it when needed is vital. Motivation is extremely fickle. It comes and goes and when it goes, it can be difficult to find again. Some people never quite find it again, or they hit rock bottom first and the pain serves as the motivation they need. When you live with high expectations, your rock bottom is higher up than that of everyone elses. Your rock bottom is self disappointment, it's self punishment, and feeling like you let yourself down AGAIN. There is little room for extended periods of motivation lulls, you must get back into the game and give yourself a chance to win. We aren't perfect. The goal isn't to be perfect, but to achieve being perfectly effective. High personal expectation is a gift and a curse. There is a side of it that provides us with unlimited focus and ambition. The other side causes us to tear ourselves down when we don't perform well enough.

Execution matters. However, there is no universal consensus on what execution is. While there are various definitions, executing can look different based on our goals and aspirations. If you are never on time to work because you fail to plan your mornings accordingly, executing for you could simply be making it in on time. Actually being effective, working diligently, providing value, and getting your job done is a different level of execution. Getting to work on-time increases your chances of executing on all the other tasks, but it all starts with how and when you show up. Stack your wins, execute on the small things consistently, build up the belief that you CAN, that you are capable of making things happen.

Momentum is a powerful force if captured at the right time. When a basketball player is making all of their jump-shots, everyone knows to feed that person because they have momentum, it's their time because they have the hot hand. When we execute consistently, the universe will keep feeding us new problems to solve, new tasks, and new ideas. We have the hot hand, we've captured the momentum, and now things aren't as difficult as we made it seem. This brings me to my next point about execution.

••

"When you change the way you look at things, the things you look at change" - Wayne Dyer

••

CLARITY

Before I understood how important it was to execute and make things happen, I dealt with so much self disappointment. My perspective was all messed up. I thought that if I just worked hard and showed up everyday I would "eventually" execute. While working hard and being present are huge requirements for being effective, they didn't result in me executing to the level I was confident I could.

The biggest reason was my struggle with clarity. I never quite knew what I wanted. I wanted to be successful, I wanted to be good, but I couldn't describe what these things were. In some cases, I eventually figured out how to be effective. It took me longer than the average person, but I got it. Still, I felt satisfied instead of accomplished, being good or above average was my steady pace. I would look at others who are able to accomplish greatness and compare myself knowing that I too had what it took to achieve those levels but somehow I never asked for help or formulated a plan. I had high expectations, a great work ethic, but an average execution level. I was looking at things all wrong. I would spend a lot of time on what the results were and how they looked. I was infatuated with the win, and victory laps played over and over again in my head but when it was time to settle down and embrace the process I couldn't.

In college I lost my way, but before my junior year I was reminded by Inky Johnson that the "process was more important than the product." He reminded me that who I became during the journey was more important than actually reaching the destination.

While the destination is important to reach, I learned that along the way there are small periods of execution that are needed. Inky Johnson was the first person I heard someone say that you cannot "cheat the grind', that you get what you're willing to give for your dreams. I was cheating the grind. Working hard was my thing, but I often looked for shortcuts to propel ahead. Those shortcuts were the cause of my disappointment. I started to understand why I lacked fulfillment when I reached the end, why something never quite felt right. I began looking at the process more closely and not the product.

Quickly I learned that the reward was truly in the becoming. It was there where I met important people and discovered vital lessons. I stopped looking at major tasks in my life from the outside in, and I began seeing them from the inside out. In the game of football you learn this early on, so it wasn't that I didn't know it, but I had lost my way over the years. It is common to lose our way or forget important small lessons people teach us so that we can be effective executors. We become intrigued by quick fixes, shortcuts, and instant gratification. While we always can appreciate those things, our foundations needs to be strong. The mindset anchoring us needs to be one that is committed to the execution of small necessary tasks regardless of their difficulty level.

In football you prepare for about 28-36 weeks out of the year for only 11 week of guaranteed 60 minute games. Most sports, organizations, or systems have the same structure. The actual time of performance is an extremely small fraction compared to the preparation. Committing our mindset to execution means that the focus is no longer the big performance, but instead treating the preparation as small necessary performances. Proper preparation was what I need to be reminded of, and though I still have moments where I struggle with it, I acknowledge that it's the most important aspect of growth.

There is a term in sports that goes "CHAMPIONSHIPS ARE WON IN THE OFFSEASON". Life has granted you with many off-seasons. Everyday that the spotlight isn't on us is an opportunity to become better and heal ourselves.

This step is about committing to execution, and it will likely be the commitment we struggle with the most because we cannot do it all ourselves. While the greatest fight is within us, we will need to find sources of encouragement, motivation, and discipline. I will remind you to utilize your resources and not allow your ego to prevent you from getting the necessary assistance. Not asking for help when I desperately needed it has been the greatest regret in my young life, and I don't want you to feel the same disappointment. YOU GOT THIS! MAKE THINGS HAPPEN!

Chapter 15:

"I'M OK"

"Im Ok" -Jose Duncan Jr.

34 days prior to being released, I was standing in a
NorthWell Health Hospital's Intensive Care Unit shocked and
confused. I stood there listening to the hospitals pastor recite the
final words of prayer as my stepmother slowly passed away.
Standing there was my dad, my stepsister, and my girlfriend. I felt
like I was suffocating because trying to hold back emotions made
it hard to breathe. The room was cold and dark, like a scene from a
sad movie. Everyone in the hospital unit knew what was
happening. Their kind word and well wishes were very comforting.
I imagined they were dealing with this reality a few times a month.
The day before my stepmother died, she made me promise to make
it to training camp and to do my best. I also promised her that I

would look after my dad and step sister if anything was to happen to her. Somehow she knew that conversation would be the last time we talked. I promised her these things because I felt like I was capable of following through. I told her that I would get a tattoo of her on my right shoulder opposite my mother's tattoo. As hopeful as we all were, she knew that her time was close.

When we all went home the previous night, she had signed a *Do Not Resuscitate Form* to ensure that if she went into cardiac arrest that she would not be resuscitated. I understood her reasoning, being ill and living in pain must have been a battle everyday. She fought everyday just to see us, and we came everyday to honor her fight. I felt that she was tired of fighting everyday, and it broke my heart because I could see the pain in her eyes each day we came to visit. She could barely speak, but she would smile. She hated the hospital food and asked me to keep it a secret when she didn't eat all of it. I loved her so much, and we both knew the last two months were the most connected we've ever been. Two years prior, I lost my mother in very similar circumstances--she too died in an ICU from a stroke and didn't want to be resuscitated either. Her death left me regretful because I had spent years hating her and we never had the conversations that were necessary to find resolve. We weren't as close as my stepmother and I, but I loved her very much as well. They both knew what real pain was. I had no idea.

Watching the two most important women in my life die in front of me changed me in ways that I struggle to express, and I prefer not to speak about here. In many ways I learned what's important in life, and at the same time I've come to realize that just being *alive* is not living. 48 hours after the passing of my stepmother I was on a plane to pursue my dreams, and today I will admit that I was not ok.

IM NOT OK

I'm sure some may think that we gain extreme motivation to make them proud after losing someone. I desperately wanted to do well, but grief had other plans. While I wanted to feel the drive to make my stepmom proud, I didn't feel it. Life became confusing and depressing. Football had already saved me from spiraling numerous times in my life, and when I was in camp, I thought it was doing it again. Some days it felt like the perfect prescription for the pain, and other times I felt like I was escaping. During downtime, I'd always wonder how my dad and stepsister were holding up. Talking about death was still an uncomfortable conversation growing up. Grief is tricky; we all express it in different ways. On the field, I began holding back, which created feelings of uncertainty about my ability to perform. In football, hesitation and uncertainty are the two things that will either get you hurt or put you out of a job. The painful reality was that it did both for me. In practice my mind wandered, and one time I zoned out so bad I missed an opportunity to get reps because I didn't hear the coach calling my name.

We all have experienced those moments where our mind goes completely away from our present reality. Sometimes we need this to cope, but other times it can be incredibly distracting. Have you ever tried to play it cool but inside you were burning, I mean *deeply* burning? Emotionally I was hurting, and I never really allowed myself to express emotion in the past, so I did what I had always done: compartmentalize. I internalized the pain. I had many opportunities to talk to teammates about it but I felt I was going to burden them with my story. I never wanted to give someone else my pain and I still don't, but today I think differently.

I've come so far that I am willing to share this pain right here in these pages to you. When you have suffered in silence and tore yourself down for so long, it begins to feel routine. The worst thing I ever got used to was internalizing everything, the good and the bad. I wouldn't get too high, but I allowed myself to be extremely low. Only when I was low did I feel like I could rise again. Yet when I did rise again, I didn't believe I deserved it. Over time I became my worst enemy. We all become our worst enemies at some point.

··

"Until the pain of staying the same is greater than the pain of change, then you will never change." - Unknown

··

'ONE DOOR CLOSES, ANOTHER…'

On January 31, 2018 I looked down at my watch to see the time. It read 11:41PM. My plane from San Antonio was pulling into JFK airport. When I went to lock my phone and store it in my bag, I accidentally took a screenshot of my lock- screen which is how I can recall the time of landing. I remember how disappointed I felt during the plane ride home after being released hours earlier. I stared out the window the entire time wondering what life was going to be like now back in NYC. I thought of my mom and stepmom the entire flight and I knew I didn't keep my word. I had let them down. My dreams of playing in the NFL slowly slipped away. I felt like I was letting down so many people.

The sad truth was that the fire in my heart no longer burned the same for the game and it scared the hell out of me. I wasn't sure what that meant. All the years of sacrifice and hard work, and it finally broke me. The thing I loved most in this world no longer had a place for me. At least, that's what I wanted to so desperately believe. The truth had become harder to accept. Getting off the flight I knew right away that I needed to accept who I had become.

I needed to accept where I was in my life, and most of all I needed to accept I wasn't where I wanted to be. Living with all the self disappointment and pressure was eating away at my happiness, and it was time for change.

I always felt like whatever unhappiness I was feeling I deserved, because I caused so many issues growing up. I caused anger, stress, disappointment, and heartbreak, and maybe the universe was repaying me. So I took it, stored it away in my mind, and kept proceeding. This time was different. The storage had finally run out, I was exposed with nowhere to hide. Everything began resurfacing all at once the following day after I returned home as if it was planned my entire life. I was so messed up emotionally, negative thoughts continued reproducing in my mind. That day I mindlessly scrolled through social media to distract myself from it all. After about 4 hours of flicking through Instagram, I came across a video of Will Smith speaking. In the interview he said something, and the moment I heard it I thought the universe was speaking directly to me.

Do you ever have those moments when you feel like the universe is speaking to you? At your lowest points, you're given a sign, and only you can interpret it the way it needs to be interpreted. That very sign could mean absolutely nothing to the person beside you because their struggle is not yours. The sign I received was so profound that I pulled out a notebook and wrote the words at the top of a new sheet of paper. It had taken some time, but those words are now serving as one of the most important reminders that I repeat to myself today.

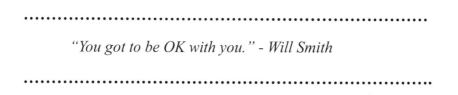

"You got to be OK with you." - Will Smith

THE ROOT OF THE PROBLEM

We deprive ourselves of the joy that we desire because we feel like we don't deserve it, but we so desperately deserve it and deep down we recognize this. When does the disappointment stop? When do we live up to our expectations without fearing success? When do we forgive ourselves? When do we sacrifice our egos so that we can learn again? When do we let it all go so that we can build anew?

We do it by admitting that we DO NOT KNOW EVERYTHING! The majority of our disappointment stems from being over-confident about what we know or what we are capable of. Oftentimes, we don't take into account that we need help until we experience below average outputs. Some of us will act like we know over and over again until we fail miserably. We set and maintain high expectations because we are confident that we know enough to do well. We become sure of ourselves because we've always been better than the average person. Everyone needs help, and if you need to be reminded of it, then you need it the most. When I say you, I mean US.

It's okay to not know. We must be ok with admitting we know nothing at all even if we do know, because only then we can welcome new energy into our life. When I decided to be OK with who I was and what I didn't know, I opened my mind and allowed for new knowledge to penetrate it. The greatest fight we face is within us, but let me remind you again, you DO NOT NEED TO FIGHT ALONE. As you continue to face your own battles, stay the course and remain diligent because you will soon find out that everyone is at war too.

You are exactly where you need to be. You have faced years of fighting off disappointment and discouragement and yet you are still standing. As time passes, we build prisons in our mind and we live in it everyday. As trapped as we feel at times, the hard truth is only we can free ourselves. My aim is to encourage you to set your mind free. Disappointment can leave us powerless, so let's take the power back. If we believe we can't, we can't, but if we believe we can, we can. I have always believed that it was possible, but the struggle has always been the HOW. The higher the expectations, the greater the risk and the bigger the effort needed to achieve it.

Everything changed when I learned how to break the big things down into 1000 pieces of smaller actions. The question of who you are versus who you want to be requires intentional and deliberate action. The truth is, you are already the person you want to be, and only time can reveal that person to the world. Sometimes life feels like an elaborate game and everyone is given a chance to play.

••

There are no rules, only moral understandings.

••

We create the rules, we make it unfair, and we create stress that isn't real. This has been our way of life for years. As we elevate, so does the pressure from society to adjust and adapt. I ask you to remain grateful, and to find peace with your past decisions and the harm done onto you. All things considered, you're ok. You're ok because you need to be, and the world needs you to be ok. We cannot afford to lose your future impact due to self disappointment causing you to forget the greatness you possess.

Do not allow others to convince you that you're not ok. Others' insecurities can sometimes enable the discouragement we already feel. Refrain from allowing others' standards to cause you to question your own. If you have insecurities and self perceived limitations, then it's time to raise your personal expectation. It's very possible your expectations for yourself are extremely low and your efforts could be reflecting as such.

A REMINDER

We all find ourselves on both sides of the coin: one moment we are ok and the next moment we feel as if we are drowning. The game is in the mind; it has always been. This final step is about making the commitment to yourself that it doesn't matter what happens, you accept who you are and what you've become. It is not final, you can change it, you can do better. You are more than enough, you may not know everything there is to know, and that's ok. A lifelong search to know everything will take 100 lifetimes, therefore that journey will not serve you in this lifetime. Instead, go all-in on your passions. Seek education around your interest and apply what you learn. Audit your life daily, run down the list of your choices, and decide which decisions you could have implemented a different perspective. Accept that other individuals think differently than you; the world works best this way.

It's ok to be open.

It's ok to be vulnerable.

It's ok that you aren't always right.

It's ok that you don't have a plan, but it's not if you stay this way.

It's ok to have faith.

It's ok that everything is not ok.

I PROMISE YOU THAT CLARITY WILL COME WITH TIME. YOU ARE OK. YOU ARE EXACTLY WHERE YOU NEED TO BE TO BECOME THE BEST VERSION OF YOURSELF.

Part Three Summary

Commitment

"I want to stop transforming and just start being." - Ursula Burns

Overcoming self disappointment has taken a lot of work and reflection. I would love to tell you that I have mastered this skill, but the truth is every now and then I have down moments. Although I still experience the disappointment, I have made a conscious decision to not punish myself for not upholding my expectations. It's ok to be unhappy with your production and performance--after all, you didn't put in all the work to fail. Commitment is all about saying no to self punishment and choosing to elevate our thinking instead.

Inky Johnson is a motivational speaker I have spoken about in a previous chapter who once said, "life touches all of us, no one is above adversity." This statement is so true in the sense that we all are going to experience disappointment. Difficult challenges affect everyone and not one person you or I know is immune to them no matter how great their lives seem. However, how we respond will have the greatest impact on our long term fulfillment with ourselves. Commitment is about having standards and expectations. We finally decide that regardless of the circumstance, we remain committed to doing what is necessary to achieve excellence.

Our primary commitment to ourselves is to SHOW UP. Our presence is sometimes all we need to create momentum. Many individuals may have catalyst personalities and are able to generate action once he or she has entered an environment.

Our second commitment is one of understanding. We must accept that pain has a place in our growth. The disappointments we experience serve a larger purpose and it's up to us to decide what purpose it serves and how it can serve us.

Our third commitment is deciding that we are capable and willing to do the hard things. Difficult tasks increase our ability to problem solve and think critically. With these skills, we can overcome any obstacle in our way. Sometimes we don't realize it, but those very obstacles in our way were put there by us, they are generated by our poor decisions.

Our fourth commitment may be one of the most important ones I have learned, especially writing this book, and that is EXECUTION. It's important that we see things through. Getting things done should be a priority. It doesn't need to be perfect, perfection is the opinion of those who are consuming it, and that you cannot control. Execution is about consistently making the right decision and how effective we are at completing important tasks.

Our final commitment is to always remind ourselves that we are ok. We need to be ok with ourselves before we expect others to be ok with us. Acceptance of who we are is important so that we can become who we desire to be without holding back. Good or bad, if you are still standing, then you still have a chance, you're still in the fight. None of these commitments will serve you if you aren't ok with yourself. I'm not asking you to alway be excited about who you are, although it helps to be excited and optimistic. I'm simply asking that you practice acceptance and reflection as these practices will provide you with enough clarity to break out of the prison you created in your mind.

Commitment by definition is "the state or quality of being dedicated to a cause, activity, etc." This practice in your journey is a promise to dedicate yourself to becoming your own hero, your own role model, and overcoming the disappointments along the way without sacrificing your expectations.

This is a You versus You situation. It always has been and always will be. Good luck!

REFLECTION

Take a moment to think about something you enjoyed about my story or the lessons in my journey. Was there anything that you could relate too? Was there moments where you could fully understand where I was coming from, or what I was experiencing?

Many of us face similar circumstances and although the contexts may differ, the lessons we learn are the same. I haven't met one person who hasn't dealt with self disappointment, self punishment, and self sabotage. We expect so much of ourselves. Belief in our abilities is not the issue and many can argue that our strong trust in those abilities is naive. It's important to note that after all the disappointment, you're still here, you're still reading this, you're still in the fight.

I named this book *The Greatest Fight Within* because the greatest fight for me has always been myself. The goal is to win small battles, overcoming losses, and finding a way to win again. The battle isn't won until you no longer punish yourself, but instead accept the reality and form a plan of action to do better.

Self awareness was the foundation I needed to reclaim my mind. In that self awareness I spent hours in deep reflection of my childhood, my parents, my family, and my life as an athlete. As a young kid, teenager, and young adult, I was constantly on the move, going through the school system and figuring myself out so I didn't spend a lot of time in reflection. Today, reflection helps me bring to surface my true emotions and experiences and allows me to find correlations between who I was and what I have become. During reflection, I started to make sense of my childhood, the teachings of my parents, and why I became the athlete that I did.

Football was always a significant part of my life and today I carry years of knowledge and wisdom from my time playing with my brothers. Being a part of something bigger than myself was a difficult journey, but today I have the utmost appreciation for organizations that function as a team. As I dug deeper into my past, I was able to understand at what points my mindset shifted, what events caused this shift, and who the individuals were that greatly influenced the change. Many of those individuals I have contacted after I stopped playing and thanked them personally for their impact on my life.

I think that telling the people in your life that you appreciate what they mean to your life is important because it serves as validation to that individual that their contributions are felt. As I transition to what I want to become and accomplish in this lifetime, I have realized that without a commitment to a few essential practices, I may not stand a chance. Therefore, I have created a few non- negotiable standards that allow me to be at my best more often. Commitment to the practices you have read about have allowed me to strive freely without fearing that self disappointment will once again steal my joy.

My personal expectations have been restored because today I am willing to do the difficult work necessary to execute. Although I strive for excellence, I remind myself to not allow perfection to stop me from creating and growing.

Although this fight is within, I did not fight it alone. I was blessed to be in environments where growth was expected by mentors and leadership that was in place. I urge you to seek high standard environments, to surround yourself with forward thinkers and leaders. If left completely alone, the fight will feel like it can never be won.

I wrote this book for you to understand my journey with living with self disappointment and high expectation. In that understanding, I hope you are able to reflect on your own journey and how you got to where you are now. You need to be willing to stand and fight. It doesn't matter what it takes or how long it takes to defeat the part of you that is holding you back from excellence.

The time is now. Take some of the lessons in this book and carry them into battle with you. I won't let you down, I promise.

APPENDIX

QOUTES USED IN THE TEXT

"The battles that count aren't the ones for gold medals. The struggles within yourself—the invisible, inevitable battles inside all of us—that's where it's at."

"The triumph can't be had without the struggle."

"I always fight with my brother. This is our way of saying I love you."

"Being able to communicate with people is power."

" I am who I am because I had to become this way."

"Start where you are, with what you have.."

"You're already in pain, get something out of it."

"Consistency is key."

"Dust yourself off, any try again."

"Know where your help is.."

"Sometimes we do not know what we don't know."

"You have to be able to accept failure and get better."

"What you're thinking is what you're becoming."

"I've got to keep showing up every day and putting in work."

"Pain is weakness leaving the body."

"It doesn't get easier, we get better."

"Some people want it to happen, some wish it would happen, others make it happen."

"Im Ok."

"I want to stop transforming and just start being."

"The longer you attempt to avoid the guilt and self-harm you have done onto yourself, the more difficult the healing process will be."

"It doesn't matter what powers you may feel you possess-- correcting the past is beyond our capabilities."

"Life is fair because it's unfair to everyone."

'Nobody likes a critic without a solution."

"Your brain is a toolbox, filled with tools you've collected over time."

"Whatever you think you need, you already have in you to get started."

"There is power in repetition, and with enough practice, you can hone this skill and use it as a superpower."

"Don't give up on yourself. If you cannot find the courage to believe in YOU, then no one will."

"If you have another shot at it, then make that next one your best."

" Never underestimate what you know, and with the help of what others know, you can be unstoppable."

"The truth is a hard pill to swallow."

"People don't fail because they aim too high and miss, but because they aim too low and hit."

"80 percent of success in life is just showing up."

"The truth is, the world isn't counting on you."

"You're already in pain, get something out of it."

"You chose the hard road the moment you decided to go after your dreams."

"If you think you can, you can."

"You never know how strong you are until being strong is your only choice."

"When you change the way you look at things, the things you look at change."

"Until the pain of staying the same is greater than the pain of change, then you will never change."

"You got to be OK with you."

"There are no rules, only moral understandings."

Acknowledgements

Thank you, **Jose Duncan Sr. (Dad),** for teaching me toughness and how to answer the door when opportunity knocks.

Thank you, **Marilyn Adolph Duncan (Stepmother),** for loving my brother, and I like we were your own. You helped get me to football camp every year and always made sure we had everything we needed. You were the glue that held the family together, holidays will never be the same. Rest in Paradise. I love and miss you everyday.

Thank you, **Barbara Stevenson (Mother),** for allowing me to become the man I've become. Thank you for giving me life.

Thank You, **Jenna Adolph,** for being my sister; every brother needs an annoying sister. I will be here to support you always. I love you.

Thank you, **Alvina Koon,** for supporting me always. You always gave me the critical feedback I needed to grow; you are unique.

219

Thank you, **Bill Solomon**, for teaching me football and the importance of being a leader. I owe you a lifetime of respect for starting the Brooklyn Titans Organization.

Thank you, **Danny Landberg**, for giving me 100-second chances to be a better student, player, and leader. Thank you for finding me and working tirelessly to get me to college.

Thank you, **Coach Carpenter,** for teaching me the power of repetition.

Thank you, **Joe Coniglio,** for coaching with your heart and proving that you wanted the best for your players every day. Thank you for being the example of a family man.

Thank you, **Pete Rektis,** for your wisdom, patience, and honest feedback. I still live by some of your sayings.

Thank you, **Bernard Thomas**, for seeing past my poor behaviors and investing your time in my success as a student.

Thank you, **Jim Fleming,** for taking a chance on a young kid from Brooklyn, NY. A full scholarship to college was always a dream of mine, and you gave that to me. Thank you for giving me the room to evolve as a leader.

Thank you, **Rudolph Bentley**, for being yourself. You always gave the best advice to football players in high school.

Thank you, **Coach Mouse**, for connecting me with great opportunities. You always advocated for me and my abilities to play football.

Thank you, **Coach Jean**, for giving me a second chance when I almost got kicked out of high school for fighting. You took a chance on me; I can't thank you enough.

To all my **former teammates**: you all taught me what it was like to be a part of brotherhood and represent something greater than myself; thank you.

Below is a list of the thought leaders, motivational speakers, and mentors I studied along my personal growth journey. They have all inspired me to take full accountability for my life and reminded me to strive for excellence. Please visit joseduncanjr.com to find some of my other work and content.

Eric D. Thomas, Ph.D. is an American motivational speaker, author and minister. Check out the *The Guru Story* on YouTube

Tony Robbins is an American author, coach, motivational speaker, and philanthropist.

Inky Johnson is an American motivational speaker and former college football player.

Justin Suah is a professional mental performance coach, author and podcaster. Listen to *Increase Your Impact* on Apple Podcasts

Brendon Burchard is a #1 New York Times best-selling author and "the world's leading high performance coach".

(High Performance Habits: How Extraordinary People Become That Way.) **Jen Sincero** *is an American writer, speaker and success coach.*

(You Are a Badass: How to Stop Doubting Your Greatness and Start Living An Awesome Life.)

Tom Bilyeu is an entrepreneur and the founder of Impact Theory University

Good luck on your journey!

Made in the USA
Middletown, DE
20 January 2021